IT'S MY AMERICA TOO

BEN FERGUSON

IT'S MY AMERICA TOO

A Leading Young Conservative
Shares His Views on Politics
and Other Matters of Importance

William Morrow *wm* *An Imprint of* HarperCollins*Publishers*

HarperCollins books may be purchased for educational, business, or sales promotional use. For information please write: Special Markets Department, HarperCollins Publishers Inc., 10 East 53rd Street, New York, NY 10022.

FIRST EDITION

Printed on acid-free paper

Library of Congress Cataloging-in-Publication Data

Ferguson, Ben, 1981–
    It's my America too : a leading young conservative shares his views on politics and other matters of importance / Ben Ferguson.—1st ed.
        p. cm.
    ISBN 0-06-059011-4
    1. Ferguson, Ben, 1981– 2. Radio broadcasters—United States—Biography.
    3. Conservatism—United States. I. Title.

PN1991.4.F47A3 2004
791.4402'8'092—dc22
[B]   2004046089

04 05 06 07 08 WBC/RRD 10 9 8 7 6 5 4 3 2 1

To my family who told me
dreams do come true.

To the critics who fuel my fire,
the skeptics who keep me going,
and those who hope I fail.

To democracy, free speech, and those
who defend the rights of this country.

This book is dedicated to you.

Life is too short to complain so make something with what you have.—Unknown

If it weren't for the last minute, nothing would get done.
—Unknown

Remember Ben, D is for diploma!—My favorite teacher

Half of the American people have never read a newspaper. Half never voted for president. One hopes it is the same half.—Gore Vidal

Keep away from people who try to belittle your ambitions. Small people always do that, but the really great make you feel that you, too, can become great.—Mark Twain

Adversity causes some men to break; others to break records.
—William A. Ward

A real leader faces the music, even when he doesn't like the tune.
—Unknown

Imagination is more important than knowledge. Knowledge is limited. Imagination encircles the world.
—Albert Einstein

Contents

PART II: TELLING IT LIKE IT IS

PART III: A POLITICAL VIRGIN

PART IV: HEROES AND ANTI-HEROES

Acknowledgments

To my dad, Bruce, the most patient man I have ever known, who has been my mentor through many fun years of "boy school." You are the one who taught me how to mow the lawn, build anything, water ski, work on cars, roof a house, drive a car, and complete numerous other tasks. Daily, your gift for service is exhibited in the way you treat friends and strangers. Unconditional is your love as is mine for you.

To my mom, Karen, who is my toughest critic and my most loyal fan. Thank you for keeping me grounded. My strengths will continue to overcome my weaknesses with your guidance, support, and love. From your son, I love you.

To my sister, Holly, who has been there since my beginning. We've played together, traveled together, spent holidays together, argued together, and survived the teenage years together. May we always be there for each other. I only hope my children have schoolteachers as dedicated as you are to teaching America's youngest! Holly, you truly are an unsung hero of American society. To my sister, the most unselfish person I know, your BIG BROTHER loves you.

To my grandfather, John Ferguson, and his wife, Doris. Thank you for your love, support, and encouragement. A special thanks for letting me drive the four-wheeler faster than my mom and dad would have let me.

To my grandfather, Charles Kenneth Robinson, who was a member of the greatest generation who ever lived. You are a great example of a leader. Thank you for introducing the game of golf to me; however, for the hours of mental golf frustration you have inflicted upon me, you will not be forgiven.

To my late grandmother, "Tot" Robinson. How I wish she could have been on earth longer. Numerous were her prayers for me and valuable were her lessons to me. Grandmother taught me at a young age to "be as honest as the day is long." I was almost eleven when she died, but her wisdom will be with me for the rest of my life.

Thank you to the Robinson family, the James family, the Shaw family, the Krenz family, the Ferguson family, and the Ragan family. You have all played an important part in my life.

To the many who have supported me, encouraged me, and prayed for me. Thank you to my dear friend Jennifer and the Yoakum family, all of your love and support is forever appreciated. To my second family, Jim, Libby, Emily, and Bo Ladyman, thanks for being in my life. To Cherry Holden and Paul Stanley who first invited me on their radio show at age thirteen, thank you so much for believing in me. To the FAFA's, remember to be nice to the little FAFA's because we are the ones who pick your retirement home.

To my church and family friends; Chrysalis participants; the faculty and families from Westminster Academy; Mark Bran, my long-time tennis coach; and the many Kappa Alpha fraternity brothers at Ole Miss, you have all played a major part in my life. To my former junior-high pastor and mentor, Don Warren, thank you for investing in my spiritual growth.

To Angie Tyson who always helps me look my best for television appearances. To Dale Jerden, thanks for being a great boss and friend.

To my best guy friends: Paul S., Paul P., Josh W., Ruffin L., Ben A., Wes G., Ben P., Jonathan F., Gene D., Bo L., and William A. You are all constant friends who keep me accountable in my walk with Christ and life. I am blessed to be able to call you my friends. I just hope I am in your weddings before my own. Don't worry, Josh, we know you are going to be the first to go.

To my best girl friends: Jennifer, you are an amazing woman; to Caroline H., Molly R., Molly M., Katie B., Neely L., Kristen W., Michael A., Rachael T., Anna B., Emily L., and Elizabeth S. Thank you for all being examples of what a solid woman is.

Special thanks goes to those who have taught me through the years. Mrs. Gibson, Mrs. Perry, and Mr. and Mrs. Carpenter, thank you for literally spending hundreds of hours outside the classroom to get me ready for college. I owe you for my success.

To my college teachers at Ole Miss: Mrs. Stone, you are the best there is; to Dr. Braseth, Dr. Husni, Dr. Albritton, Dr. Bullion, Mr. Wilkie, and Mrs. Robertson, thank you for teaching me and most importantly believing in me. You have made my college years a learning experience.

To Radio America, thank you for judging my talent and not my age. Thanks to Steve G. for your guidance; to Mike P., Peter T., Jim R., and BQ, you are all a joy to work with.

To Wendy Guarisco and her family, you are the best publicist I have ever known. Thank you for betting on me. Without you I would not be where I am today.

To Lisa Queen, my literary agent at IMG, thank you for being my ambassador to the book world. You never gave up on me even when all others thought I could not do this. You are proof that there is still integrity in corporate America.

To Henry Ferris at William Morrow, thank you for your support, confidence, and belief in me. Most importantly thank you for taking time out of your day several years ago to meet with a young kid visiting a big city.

To Michael Morrison and Sharyn Rosenblum at HarperCollins, it has been a pleasure and blessing to work with the best in the business.

To Steve Kettmann, thank you for helping me turn my thoughts into words on the page. Without your gift this book would have not been what it has become.

To Beverly Rainey, thank you for all your hard work and late nights making sure all my thoughts came across in a clear concise voice.

Thank you to my radio friends and mentors, Nate Lundy, Ken Hamblin, Drew Anderson, Kit Carson, Michael Reagan, Ray and Jennifer Steele, Mike Fleming, Sean Hannity, and Rush Limbaugh. Thank you all for your help and advice.

Thank you to all my radio listeners, guests, radio stations, and their program directors. You have played a vital role in my career and have encouraged me to pursue my goals, passions, and hopes for this country.

To CNN, Fox News, MSNBC, CNBC, thank you to all the bookers who have booked me on the air. You proved that anyone can have a voice if they try hard enough. You all took a chance when I was younger to put me on the air, and I thank you for that.

To David Webb at Sonlight Studios, thank you for making the best promo video I have ever seen. You make me look good on TV and that, my friend, shows how good you really are.

Thank you to all the people who judged me on my ability and did not pre-judge me on my age. You are the ones who make this country great. Please don't ever lose your ability to think outside the box and let others be heard.

Finally, I want to thank God for putting the people listed above in my life. I will never take these opportunities for granted.

Introduction

I could talk all day and all night and into next week about everything I love about being an American. But you know what? Pride in your country can never be a passive experience. We can't just sit back in our recliners and say, "Yep, we rule!" If we do, this country will find itself continuing to head in the wrong direction and going there in a big hurry. The real question is why we continue to trust the politicians and the other powers that be to look out for regular people like you and me.

Almost any poll will tell you that Americans just don't trust politicians. Heck, it seems that Americans can't stand politicians in general. I am writing this book to encourage everyone to help take back what is rightfully ours. The time has come to decide that we are going to band together and make some serious noise. You should know I am a conservative, and *I don't like what the Democrats stand for.* If still, after you read this book, you don't like conservatives, then please by all means fight against what I believe in. The bottom line is, get involved and be heard.

You might think I've got some very powerful people backing me up. Where else would I get my confidence? Well, that's just not the case. I get my confidence from being close to God. No, I am not a Bible beater. In fact, I hardly talk about God in this book. But you should know that the foundation of my beliefs comes from my strongly held faith in God. I also believe in old-fashioned family values. And I believe in respecting my elders because there is a lot we can learn from them.

I am lucky enough to have been raised in a quiet community in Memphis, Tennessee, where I learned that no one should ever have to apologize for being close to their family. My parents are a huge part of who I am. They taught me that sometimes you have to stand up and be counted. They taught me that we need to make sure our voices are heard. We have the right and responsibility to clear our throats and speak out loudly and clearly so all the leaders of this country can hear us when we tell them, "It's my country too!"

I am proud to say I believe in God. I am proud to say I believe in people. I am proud to say I believe in the American dream. It's time we all start to believe in who we are and stop listening to people in Washington who tell us they know what's best for us. I wrote this book because I wanted to inspire others to let themselves be heard. I am living proof that anyone—and I do mean anyone—can make a difference. You will never know if you don't give it a try. Take it from me, it feels good. Actually, it feels *great*. For me, there's nothing more fun than going on TV and debating someone like Janeane Garofalo who thinks she's some big expert on world affairs and politics. Last I checked she was only an actress and comedian. The war in Iraq was one of the saddest things I ever saw. Before the war, very few Americans had even heard of Janeane Garofalo or the guy who made that movie *Bowling for Columbine,* Michael Moore. And very few Americans ever sat around listening to the music of Moby, another half-famous Hollywood activist who decided that all of a sudden he was qualified to tell the American people that we should not go to war. Mike Farrell, Susan Sarandon, and Tim Robbins were just a few of the other Hollywood types who joined the club to argue that we should let Saddam Hussein continue torturing his own people. These are the people who inspire me to make a difference. These Hollywood liberals don't know anything about war. They have no background in foreign relations, and I'd bet you money they couldn't tell you how the United Nations actually operates. But even so, they backed the UN in its opposition to the war, and they backed the liberal movement against George W. Bush. But in reality they were backing Saddam. I am sick and tired of these people influencing my generation. It's people my age—not older Americans— who say to themselves, "Hey, they're famous; let's back their cause." If I've got one goal, it's to let my generation know how they are being used by these famous Hollywood types, the powerful Washington types, and the anti-American types.

The second reason I am writing this book is to show people that being a conservative does not mean you are rich, old, and wear a sweater-vest. Being conservative is a mind-set, not a lifestyle, and I am living proof of that. Sure, some conservatives can be as boring as heck, but I still like the conservative ideas and that's why I believe in them. What I don't like are liberals like Ted Kennedy or Howard Dean who bash the right wing with criticisms that don't even add up. These Democrats run around thinking they are better than the rest of us, and they think people will just accept what they say, because the way they say it drips with sanctimony and holier-than-thou empathy. You would think they would have enough respect for the American people to make their case in an honest, straightforward way. Forget it. It won't ever happen. Just look at someone like Bill Maher, the host of *Real Time*. The only way he ever wins a debate is by bringing on two other liberals to fight with him, and when the conservative tries to talk, he drops the f-bomb and talks over them until the audience laughs and it looks like Maher wins. But if he really had to prove himself talking about politics, he would fall flat on his face. The only way someone like Bill Maher can win an argument is to turn it into a one-sided discussion. Liberals like one-sidedness. It empowers them. They think other liberals will tune in if you can listen to a lot of people sitting around agreeing with one another on everything. They see being a liberal as belonging to some club, and if you are part of the club, then you must be right, and everyone else must be wrong. But their arguments just don't hold up when they are exposed and discussed in detail. That is why liberals have to resort to personal attacks so often. That is why they make fun of you personally. Otherwise, if they had an audience of average Americans and not just fellow liberals, they would lose every time. I say to liberals like these: Bring it on! You can put me up against an Al Franken or a Bill Maher anytime if you take away their stage and supporting cast. Take it away and they'll lose every time. I guarantee it!

If you look at issues like gun control or affirmative action, it's clear that the only way liberals can convince you they are right is to show you a false picture of reality. Gun sales have gone up in this country since the September 11 terrorist attacks. More people own guns than ever before. So, according to the arguments we have been hearing for so long from antigun nuts, violent crime should be a raging epidemic. We should be seeing more and more murders each year. But since the facts don't bear out that argument, liberals with a thing against guns just switch to some new argument, or they try to manipulate people by using some fresh horror story pulled from the headlines.

It's the same with racial quotas. These make sense to no one, except maybe liberals who use this subject to get the minority vote. Democrats use minorities like they're going out of style. They are like the latest fashion accessory from Louis Vuitton or Brooks Brothers. And that's how they defend quotas. It amazes me that we still hear liberals arguing that because of history, we must pay past debts of discrimination by holding spots open for candidates with special qualifications. What does it take for these people to accept that this do-gooder mentality only makes things worse? If you discriminate against anyone, and deny him or her a job or a spot in school so you can give it to someone else less qualified because of the color of his or her skin, the person discriminated against will become bitter and angry. That bitterness and anger will find a way out, sooner or later. And even the people who get the special treatment have their own issues. They will always wonder if they could have done it on their own without getting special breaks.

So many issues are as clear and obvious as these two, if we would only debate them honestly. The problem is liberals never want to let this happen. I believe they are afraid that their arguments won't hold up under the public's eye. That is why it drives them crazy when someone like President Bush talks to the American people in plain English. And I'm sure the liberals go even more nuts when they see the public respond favorably. George W. Bush doesn't talk down to people. He doesn't think he is smarter than you, me, or your cousin Mabel. He's not in love with the sound of his voice. He speaks only when he has something to say.

People laughed at me when I was thirteen or fourteen and started saying I wanted to have my own radio talk show. They laughed some more when I said I wanted to go on network TV to debate the issues. But I have been on Fox News, MSNBC, CNBC, and CNN many, many times, debating a wide variety of issues. I became the youngest syndicated-radio talk-show host in the country when Radio America gave me a show on Sundays, and I am happy to say that I'm now heard on more than a hundred stations.

I have accomplished my goals with no special advantages. I didn't get my radio show because my mom or dad owned a radio station. I didn't get on national TV because my parents work for a network. And no, my grandfather is not someone like Ted Turner (thank goodness). The fact is, my parents are not rich. I got my own show because I have a perspective on my generation that is unusual among the media, and I can seriously debate on the big issues of our times. This is because I have learned to inform myself about what's going on in the world. I love newspapers, and I love history. It is only with a good sense of the past that we can learn how to plan the future. Inform yourself like I have. If you want to make a difference in America, you must study current events and history. If I can do it, you can, too.

Finally, if you read this book and it makes you angry, that's great. But don't just get mad. Do something about it. That is what needs to take place in America. We have to turn this great country around. Most politicians have no clue what the average American goes through. Sure, they have polls to tell them what we think, but I have never heard of a poll making this country a better place to live. The only way they will change is if we force them to listen. That is how we will take back what is ours, and it all starts with you.

PART I

Son of the South

CHAPTER 1

Falling in Love with Radio

I was always fascinated with radio. I guess I had an overactive imagination, because when I heard people talking on the radio, I would spend a lot of time wondering what they looked like. It was that same curiosity kids naturally have about the unknown. I think I just took it a little further. I would listen to the deejays and try to paint a picture in my head of what they looked like. Were they tall? Or short? Thin? Or fat? A mental picture would pop into my head, based on how they sounded. I would try to imagine the studio, the microphones, every detail I could put together in my head without ever having seen a studio in person.

Having time to listen to radio was one of the big advantages of home-schooling. I am sure I would never have ended up where I am now if I had not spent so much time in the family minivan driving around town with my mother while other kids were stuck in boring classrooms, staring at the walls or ripping apart their paper, piece by piece. If my mother would drive to the supermarket, I went with her. If she would drive to the post office, I went along for the ride. We spent a lot of time together, which I think was good for our relationship, and it also gave me plenty of chances to listen to the radio with her as we sat in the car. Sometimes we listened to music, but by the time I was eight years old or so, we started to listen to Rush Limbaugh's show almost every day. We'd be driving to my tennis lessons, or taking my sister to horseback riding, and along the way we would be tuned into Rush Limbaugh, who became a big influence on me.

Rush was just starting to make a splash around that time. He worked in music radio for a Pittsburgh stations in the early 1970s and even had a show for a while as "Bachelor Jeff" and "Jeff Christie," but he quit radio for a while and went to work for the Kansas City Royals baseball team as director of group sales. He was doing political commentaries on Kansas City radio but was fired from that job when they decided he was too opinionated. Imagine that! Rush daring to express his opinions! I bet those guys who decided to fire him felt like real geniuses a couple of years later when Rush was the talk of every living room in America. He moved to Sacramento to start his first talk show and did well out there. It was July 1988 when he moved to New York to start his national show, and, not much later than that, my mother and I started listening to him and other talk radio a lot.

I was pretty young, so I don't remember being impressed by his opinions, or his ideas, or his arguments. I just loved that he could keep talking and talking and talking without ever slowing down, no matter what the subject was. That was kind of my dream. He was my hero and not because I thought he was so fascinating. I was just amazed at the way he came on the air every day, and he could talk about anything he wanted. I remember thinking that I would love to do that, too. I just knew right away that it would be great to have the chance to talk about whatever I wanted to talk about every single day and have people listen to me. That idea intrigued me.

I also remember loving the fact that here Rush was, basically an unknown at that point, and he would go after anybody, no matter how big they were. That to me was cool. It wasn't like he was famous back then. It wasn't like he was a movie star. He just seemed real to me, like someone you would talk to when your parents had a bunch of neighbors over for a Fourth of July barbeque, or something like that. It's hard to explain, because now everybody knows Rush Limbaugh. But back then he was just starting out, and even then, there was this sense that you knew him, even though you had never met him. I think that's what made me feel such a strong connection to him. He was just a totally different kind of personality than the famous people I was aware of at that time, who seemed remote and untouchable somehow. You couldn't really connect with movie stars. Maybe you see them in a movie, and on the cover of *People* magazine, but you never feel any immediate sense of connection.

Don't get me wrong. I am sure I absorbed more from Rush than I will ever know. If not for him, I might not have developed such a love of undressing liberals in public by pointing out all the flaws in their arguments. I might not have learned to have quite so much fun making jokes about all the stupid things people in Washington do and say. I was always a very opinionated kid, so I was that much more interested in hearing Rush express his opinions, and I guess his enthusiasm for what he did rubbed off on me.

He was able to do what I wanted to do. I couldn't back talk to my parents out of respect. But I always tried to have a quick comeback, and I always wanted to have the last word. That was part of why I enjoyed listening to Rush so much. He was able to have the last word, and it was okay. He could be brassy and cut people off. I was impressed with the way he could control the conversation. That made a big impression on me because, when you're a kid, the older people around you establish rules and you have to play by those rules or face the consequences. You can never interrupt, and you always have to say "yes ma'am" and "no ma'am."

It really got on my nerves being treated like a kid all the time. I always liked talking to adults. My mother says that even when I was three years old, I would walk across the street to talk to a neighbor lady, Nell, whose husband had passed way. "If I let Ben, he would sit on her porch and talk with her for hours," my mother says now. "Nell once told me she didn't know how to talk to a little three-year-old, but she didn't have to worry. Benjamin would march right up her steps and say, 'Hi, can we have a visit?' and chat about anything he wanted to discuss. He would also go visit other neighbors, including an older couple next door, Sally and Edgar, who were both in the newspaper business. He swapped stories with them. He was already quite the talker."

I was the kind of kid who could sit down and have a conversation at the adult table during the holidays, but then go right back to the kids' table and fit in there just fine. But sometimes I would get frustrated because the older people were talking about the stock market or the real estate market or whatever it may have been, and I would want to jump in and join the conversation, but you don't always get heard because you're young. People laugh and say, "What a cute little kid." That really ticked me off.

Radio was my way to talk to people without being told to shut up. It dawned on me at some point that if I could call in to a show, and they put me on the air, then they were going to have to let me have my say. I started bugging my mother to let me call the Rush Limbaugh show. I had memorized the number from all the times I'd listened to the show, and I remember being really, really nervous the first time I picked up the phone to call. But I kept getting busy signals. I tried and tried, but I could never get through. It was really frustrating. Eventually I came up with the idea of calling the local station that syndicated Rush and asking them what I could do to get on his show. They said they couldn't help me get on to talk with Rush, but they recommended I try calling some other shows that weren't as popular as Rush's and didn't have so many callers.

Soon I was calling local shows all the time because then I could get through to talk on the radio. It was really entertaining for me. I liked calling into the *Mike Fleming Show* on the same local station in Memphis that picked up Rush's show. I would just call in and talk about whatever he felt like discussing. I almost have to laugh, thinking about it now, because I would be on hold waiting to talk to the host and my heart would be pounding away at ninety miles an hour. That's how nervous I was. But I guess I sounded all right on the air, because soon Mike Fleming started remembering my voice when I called.

My mother wasn't worried about my calling in to radio shows. She said I could hold my own, so if I wanted to keep calling, that was fine with her. She would usually be around when I called, and sometimes she would tape the shows so I could listen again later. Once when I was eleven or twelve years old, I called in to Mike Fleming's show when he was discussing a local politician named Harold Ford who had had a lot of legal troubles but somehow kept finding a way out. He was indicted in 1987 for receiving allegedly illegal loans, but that case ended up with a hung jury in 1990. Three years later, another jury acquitted him. Ford was one of the headliners in the congressional House banking scandal in 1993 when it came out that he had written 388 bad checks between 1988 and 1991, for a total of $552,447. I called in to say it just wasn't right that Ford was getting away with it, and I pointed out that if Ford was my age, he probably would have been sent to jail for what he had done.

"How old are you?" Fleming asked, but he asked it in a nice way.

I was just a kid, so I was the last one in the world to have any kind of perspective on what I was doing. I just did what felt right and pursued the fresh challenges as they came along. But looking back, I think I now have an advantage on the radio because of all my experiences as a teenager. More than ever, the art of debating on TV or radio is the art of never letting them see you sweat. You have to have your arguments lined up, you have to be ready with facts you can cite, and you have to know enough about what your opponents will say that you will never, ever be surprised. But come on, let's be honest here: The main thing is sounding and looking confident and relaxed and totally at ease. If I can come across in such a way that I give people the strong feeling I have been doing this my whole life, which I basically have been, that can only help. To say it's in my blood doesn't go nearly far enough. It feels closer to the truth to say it *is* my blood.

I was twelve years old the first time I made someone cry on the radio, and it was the host of the show I called. I called in to debate an issue she had been discussing that day. I told her the arguments she was using were ridiculous and rattled off about five or six facts to prove it, too. That was too much for her. She just lost it. Right there on the radio. In fact, she had to go to a commercial break so she could pull herself together and stop crying. The paper even did an article the next day talking about how she had broken down on the air. The article didn't mention me, though. I kept right on calling her show all the time. I really couldn't stand her politics. I was the only kid who called in, so people got to know my voice, and when they heard "Here's Ben from Cordova," they knew I was going to be giving her a good fight.

I don't know how anyone could stand to listen to me on the radio back then, my voice was so high. I know if I were listening, I would have switched stations in a hurry or maybe burned the radio. I hadn't hit puberty yet, so my voice was as high as a kite. I would let my mom tape me, but I never listened. It was like torture hearing my own voice. I sounded like a girl. It was awful, absolutely awful. I have no clue how anyone listened to me until I was fifteen or sixteen, but they did for some reason.

School lunch programs became a big issue for me. A bunch of Democrats showed up at the White House in 1994 for a photo op with Bill Clinton and to jab at the Republicans, saying they wanted to cut funding for school lunches. It sounded crazy to me. As soon as I heard that, I figured it would be political suicide for the Republicans to do that, and I had trouble believing they could make such a big mistake. I told my mother it was the dumbest thing I had ever heard, and she told me, "Why don't you figure it out?" So I looked into it, and what I found out was that the Republicans actually wanted to increase school lunch funding by 4.5 percent, which was almost the same as the 5.2 percent increase the Democrats favored. It was a lie to say the Republicans wanted to cut school lunch funding, and I was really mad.

That was when it hit me that this was not just a game or some kind of sport: This was how I wanted to spend my life. I was so tired of the Democrats manipulating people. They were just using kids as their backdrop. They used kids for political gain. A group was probably on some tour of the White House and they sent some operative over to ask, "Hey, do you want to be on TV?" and the kids stood back there and grinned for the cameras. But they had no clue what was going on. They had no idea of the facts. I was really upset at the way the Democrats used kids for polls and ratings, because the youth of America are the future. So when I was thirteen, I told myself: That's it. I'm going to be a spokesman for my generation.

I had a few lucky breaks along the way. When I called the local station to ask about getting on Rush Limbaugh's show, one of their suggestions was that I try calling in to Ken Hamblin, a black conservative who at that time was on more than one hundred stations around the country. He had a great voice for radio and sounded a lot like James Earl Jones. I tried calling his show, which was based in Denver, and it worked out pretty well. He put me on the air and was very nice to me, and soon I was calling in regularly. I had probably been on his show six or seven times when he decided he enjoyed having me on the air and was going to give me a nickname. I don't know how he came up with it, but he took to calling me Young Master Ben.

I would call in and he would tell his audience that he was going to talk to Young Master Ben. We would discuss something that was in the news at the time for a few minutes and that was that. We never planned it ahead of time. I just called in when the time seemed right. He gave me a special phone number to call right through to the studio, and soon I knew the names of his producer and his call screener. They would try to put me right on the air when I called, because they knew I was calling long distance and had to get permission from my parents before I called.

It developed into kind of a routine where I would call on Thursdays and they would put me on the air with Ken for fifteen or twenty minutes, sometimes even half an hour. This opportunity came out of nowhere, but soon it was almost like a real segment on his show: Thursdays with Young Master Ben. Then one week I was sick and realized I couldn't do the show. I figured it would be no problem, and no one would even notice.

But a strange thing happened. People started calling in from all over the country, asking, "Where is Young Master Ben?" or "What happened? Why isn't he on the show this week?" Ken and his producers thought this was just hysterical. They called my house right away, talked to my parents, and asked what had happened to me.

"Oh, he's fine, he's just under the weather today," my mother told them.

That was when they kind of took it to the next level. So one day when I was on the air with Ken, I said, "I have a question. How do you get into talk radio?"

"Start smoking," Ken said, joking.

That was how high my voice was at the time. It was pretty funny, because Ken had this deep, booming voice, and he was talking to this thirteen-year-old kid with a really high-pitched voice.

I thought that was funny, but I didn't like the rest of what he said. He told me to wait until I was a lot older and more mature before I gave it a shot. I said, "Thank you very much." But inside, I was thinking, "We'll see." I wanted to do it then. I really thought I was ready. I figured if I could talk about politics on the radio with Ken, I could talk about politics on the radio by myself on my own show. I probably should have been discouraged by what Ken said, and I'd probably give the same advice to a thirteen-year-old now, but at the time, I wasn't about to let him slow me down.

Another good break came when a guy named Paul Stanley called the *Ken Hamblin Show* looking for me. He had an AM political show in Memphis every afternoon Monday through Friday, along with his co-host, a woman named Cherrie Holden. Paul had been listening to me on the air with Ken and liked what he heard. He knew I was from Memphis, so he wanted to have me on his show to introduce me to the radio world. He called me at home after he got my number from Ken Hamblin.

"Hi, Ben," he said. "I have a talk show called *Inside Memphis* on 1210 AM. Would you like to come and be a guest?"

"Sure!" I told him.

So I went down there, and the first time they had me on the air, the plan was for me to be on for ten minutes. But the phone lines were jammed. I stayed on for an hour and a half, and they asked me back. My parents drove me down to the station the next day, and, again, the phone lines were jammed. So they asked me to come back the next week. I did, and, again, the calls kept coming in with people wanting to talk to me on the air. I went back one more time, and they offered me a regular job.

I was thirteen years old, and I had a regular spot on the air. Paul Stanley left the show to go work for Majority Leader Bill Frist, and now he's a Tennessee state representative. I was on pretty much every Thursday with Cherrie, depending on school, and I did that for about six months. We would talk about politics, read the morning newspaper, and hit whatever the big topics were. We didn't get too fancy about it. We would just go into the station, talk together about what to cover on the air, and then start the show, do the commentary, and take phone calls.

I was learning more about what worked on radio, and from this I formed my own ideas. Listening to Rush so often when I was younger had a big influence on me, and Rush was the one who got me excited about the immediacy and power of radio. But as much as I wanted to emulate Rush in some ways, there were certain things he did that I knew I did not want to do. I don't mean that as a criticism. Rush is the best in the business. But I learned that I am not Rush and I don't want to try to be Rush, I want to be Ben Ferguson.

One thing I learned from Rush was that it was important to be more patient with callers than he is. I must have called his show hundreds of times and heard hundreds of busy signals. One day I finally got through and waited two hours, because it was so important for me to talk directly to my mentor. I finally made it on the air and the whole call lasted maybe twenty seconds. Half of that time was Rush introducing the call. I had only a few seconds to speak, and then he got rid of me. I'll never forget what that felt like, or I hope I never will anyway. I learned that day always to keep in mind that if a caller waits an hour to talk to you, you can give him at least two minutes of your time. After all, without the callers and the listeners, you don't have a job. If these people have so much respect for you and your show that they are willing to wait so long, you can show them some respect in return.

I also learned by listening to Rush that it doesn't work so well if listeners get the idea that you think you are always right and anyone who disagrees with you must always be wrong. That's just not my personality. I don't think I am always right. It's important to me to hear people out and to listen to what they have to say, especially if they disagree with me. I might learn something. My thinking might change. Rush takes a different approach. If someone calls into his show and disagrees with him, Rush usually does not give him or her much time. I want to trade ideas with people. I want to know why they believe what they believe. I want to influence people and shape their ideas, but if I never let the other side talk, then they will turn me off forever, and I will never get a chance to influence the way they look at the world.

CHAPTER 2

Making a Splash

I found out early on that a great way to make a splash on radio was to have well-known guests on the show. That way, you could grab people's attention and hold on to it. Even when I was thirteen, doing my first show once a week with Cherrie Holden in Memphis, I always felt very comfortable talking on the air about any issue, but I also liked to have guests. People couldn't believe a thirteen-year-old kid could land interviews with a Bob Dole or a Newt Gingrich, so they really got a kick out of hearing me talk to those kinds of famous politicians. I always loved a challenge, and getting "big" guests to come on the show was a great challenge. I became known for that. It was kind of my niche.

I had fun with it, and I mean the whole thing, especially the chase. I would put in calls to press secretaries and tell them who I was and what I wanted, and at first they would think I was messing with them. A lot of times they would laugh at me. But I was always very persistent, and a lot of big-name political people were just plain intrigued by the idea of going on a radio show with a thirteen-year-old host. My first big guest was Ken Hamblin. He had to be my first guest because he had helped me so much getting into radio. Soon after that I had on a congressman named Ed Bryant. Then I pulled off a real coup by getting Senator Fred Thompson, the former lawyer and now actor. He was a good guest. He tells it like it is. Bill Frist came on the show about then, too.

Probably the most important guest I had on in those first months was a California congressman named Bob Dornan, who served nine terms in the House before losing his seat to Loretta Sanchez in 1996. Dornan was a real character, known as "B-1 Bob," who was great at talking politics in a colorful manner. He used to joke about how happy the "lesbian spear-chuckers" would be to see him lose. Dornan had a great time talking to me on my show that first time. He was in no hurry to end the call, so we just kept talking, and he got more and more interested in helping my young career along. You know how older people like to say something nice to encourage young people? Well, Bob Dornan said, "Why, you ought to bring your show on up to Washington and do it from the Capitol." That's just how politicians talk, trying to say things that sound good on the air, but I took him seriously. I just said, "Okay, sounds good—and thank you very much," and we hung up the phone. I didn't waste any time before I followed up on that. I called Dornan's office the next morning.

"Hey, you offered to help me," I said.

So he explained what I needed to do.

"If you can raise some money to pay for doing your show up here, and you can get yourself up here, I'll make sure you get to broadcast from the Capitol," he told me.

I was thrilled. "Thank you very much," I told him, and then I ran off to tell my parents.

"Look, that's going to be a lot of money," they told me. On top of our family's expenses, we would have to pay for plane tickets, hotel rooms, and the expenses of a producer and my co-hosts.

It was going to add up fast. We had to consider being in Washington for a week, paying for hotels, meals, and all that kind of stuff. I was pretty disappointed to hear it was going to be so complicated to arrange, but I wasn't about to give up. That has never been my personality. The more difficult something sounds, the more I rise to the challenge. My parents were trying to let me down easy. They were worried that I would take it hard. But I was positive about the whole idea from the beginning, and that never changed. I was flat-out sure I was going, and the only question was how to arrange it.

I kicked around some different ideas and then decided to go with what had worked before. I picked up the phone and called Ken Hamblin to ask for his advice. I explained to Ken that Bon Dornan had been on as a guest and invited me to bring the show up to Washington if I could arrange the trip. I asked Ken if he had any ideas about how I could raise the money I would need. He laughed at first, maybe because I sounded so enthusiastic, and then told me he had an idea.

"We'll go on the air and ask my listeners to help pay for the trip," he told me, and I almost dropped the phone I was so happy.

So almost every week I went on his show. It was great. I would give an update, telling people about the latest check I had received, whether it was from a wealthy listener who had sent in a couple hundred dollars or a guy in jail who sent me a buck. I had a shoebox full of letters with checks in them. People sent in checks for $5, $10, $15, $20, $100—whatever they could afford.

I knew we were going to make it when a lady called in who said she was the president of the stewardess association for TWA airlines. She said she could get us all cheap stand-by tickets for $50 a person, and she threw in my ticket for free. Somebody else contacted us who had a connection with the Sheraton and got us discounted rooms at the Sheraton Crystal City Hotel in Arlington, Virginia, less than three miles away from the center of Washington, D.C. Once we had all that arranged, it was time for me to call back Bob Dornan.

"Hey, I've got it all taken care of, when can I come?" I told him.

He was just in shock. It had never dawned on him that I could actually pull it off. But he was a good sport. He had made me a promise, and he lived up to it, and it turned into a really big deal. I couldn't believe all the doors that were opening for me. Bob Dole came down, and I interviewed him live. I always liked his sense of humor, and it came through that day. We went up to Newt Gingrich's office right after I interviewed him about the Contract with America. I remember he had this big dinosaur head and a framed copy of the Contract that had a hole punch next to each item that he had completed. That was pretty cool. Dornan came on the show, and, again, he was a great guest. I did my show from Washington for several days, and it was such a great experience for me. I had so many big names on the show that week, and Bob Dornan even invited me to come along with him when he was on Mary Matalin's MSNBC show *Equal Time,* and I ran into Newt Gingrich, who remembered me from the day before.

"Hi, Ben," he said. "What are you doing here?"

Everyone was pretty shocked that a thirteen-year-old was getting around so much. The Associated Press article that moved on the wires that morning was headlined GINGRICH WARNS LIMBAUGH OF TEEN COMPETI-TION, so everyone was wondering about me and my show. That week came at a time when the Contract with America was huge, so we talked about it all the time, and I had such a great look at Washington from the inside out. I even learned an important political lesson. Newt Gingrich promised me he was going to call up Rush Limbaugh and try to get me a gig guest-hosting for him. He even made the same promise in the AP article, and, as a thirteen-year-old, I was just sure that if he said it, he would do it. But he never did. That was a hard lesson in how empty politicians' promises can be.

My first radio show lasted about six months, and then Cherrie Holden quit to take a job working for the governor of Tennessee. That was that, I figured. I thought I would go back to my normal life and live like any other kid my age. But it must have been a slow news week or something because the day we quit, the local TV stations and the *Commercial Appeal* and *Memphis Flyer* all came out to do stories. Several radio stations called the next day to ask me about coming to work for them. So I went to the interviews dressed to impress. I would head upstairs, and my parents would wait downstairs until I finished. A 5,000-watt AM station in Memphis offered me a job talking about politics every Tuesday afternoon at two o'clock doing a show called *Mid-South Viewpoint*. I accepted, and every Tuesday I would come to the studio and get ready to do my show.

If you think about it, that was actually kind of weird. Here they were, a major commercial radio station, and they were taking a chance on a thirteen-year-old. That's something you just don't do. It was pretty foreign to them. But they wanted the media attention, and they thought it was worth taking a chance on me. That was why they approached me. They knew I could attract younger listeners to the station. It took them a while to warm up to me, but I ended up doing that show for more than two years.

People all over Memphis would tune in just to hear who I could get to come on my show. I was constantly surprising people with my guests. Lamar Alexander, Al Gore, Richard Gephardt—they were all guests on that show. Once again, I used guests to get people to listen. I loved calling people and kind of throwing a curveball at them, just by being my age and asking them to come on my radio show. I wasn't intimidated by anybody, and I think they could hear that in my voice. I would call up press secretaries and give them my age and say, "I'd like to have the Speaker of the House on my radio show," or "I'd like to have the Senate majority leader." They couldn't believe it, but a lot of times they would just say, "What the heck, we'll give him a shot."

Later, another station in the area called and offered me a three-hour show five days a week. I was only fifteen years old, but I took the job. That was a real grind. I loved doing it, but doing three hours of radio, five days a week, will really test you. It doesn't take long to find out if you have anything to say or if you know how to connect with an audience. If you are afraid, or try too hard, you will bomb and bomb fast. It was probably a good thing when the station changed formats barely six months after I started doing the show. Again, that was that.

I was ready for a break. It felt to me as if I had been doing radio shows forever by then, because that's how it is when you are sixteen. I wanted time to play basketball with friends. I wanted time to work on my tennis. So I decided not to look for another job and satisfied myself by calling nationally syndicated shows from time to time just to keep my radio reflexes sharp. But when I was seventeen, a guy who had a weekend show on the biggest news talk station in Memphis called and asked if I wanted to be his co-host. So I did that every weekend until I went to college. There was no way I could have played college tennis and kept doing the show, and I wanted to give my tennis a fair shot and see how good I could be.

One advantage of going to college was I could finally enter the Young American Broadcaster of the Year contest, which offers a $5,000 scholarship to one person every year. I entered my senior year of high school, and they told me I was not eligible to win because I was not in college yet. Otherwise, I think I could have won that year. They asked me to their convention in Washington anyway, along with seventeen other kids from around the country. My freshman year, I was eligible and thought I had a great shot. I heard the tape of the other person up for the top prize, a guy from Texas named Matt McClearin, and I figured I had a really good chance of winning. But I came in second place that year and was seriously frustrated because I had used an unedited tape, which was what they asked for in the rules, while some other contestants had entered tapes that they had edited together.

The next year I wasn't taking any chances. I called up the people behind the contest and said that if other people were going to send in edited tapes, I would do that, too. So they said they would make it very clear in the rules. If you look at the website now, they even put it in boldface: five "**unedited**" minutes of your best air check. It was very clear that it had to be an unedited script and an unedited tape from the radio. So I sent in mine, and I would have been really upset with myself if I hadn't won.

Finally the call came, and they told me, "Congratulations! You won, hands down. You get the scholarship. You are the 2002 Young American Broadcaster of the Year."

I guess the third time was a charm. I went to New York to receive the award. Blanquita Cullum invited me to come on her show, which was syndicated by Radio America. She talked me up as the winner of this contest, and we discussed some political issues on the air. The bosses at Radio America liked what they heard. They thought, Hey, this kid can hold his own. So when Blanquita went out of town, they had me do her show, and it went really well. Soon they were flying me up to Washington for more guest-hosting, like three hours a day for five days, and then they were offering me a job, even though I was only twenty-one. I was definitely the youngest syndicated-radio talk-show host in the country, and I still am now.

I would never have landed my own talk show if I had not been so lucky in getting great advice from so many top people. Ken Hamblin was very generous, as I have said, and Kit Carson also helped me out. He has been with Rush Limbaugh for years, as his producer and right-hand man, and I got his number and bothered the crap out of him ever since I was thirteen, calling all the time to say hello and asking for his advice. I was never shy about asking people for help or for advice. I would always be interested in hearing anything they had to say about how to get into radio, how to get better, what to avoid, etc., etc. I called people all the time and bothered them until they helped me out. So one time Kit Carson gave me some excellent advice.

"The reason Rush Limbaugh is so good is not because of who he has on his show, it's because of what he talks about," he told me. "If you want to separate yourself from the rest of the crowd, you have to find a way to talk by yourself the whole time and not have any guests."

He has a point. If you base it all on guests, then people are going to turn on the radio and listen to hear what guest you have on the show, and then if it isn't someone they want to hear, they flip to another station and are done with you. If you can talk about events in a conversational and entertaining way, and people tune in to hear you, then you are always going to have an audience. It won't depend so much on having a big-name guest. I kept that in mind when I was thinking about my syndicated show, and from the beginning I have kept guests to a minimum. I don't think I have had more than ten guests these last two years since I started being syndicated. I was very aware that I wanted people to listen in order to hear what I had to say. So I think that's a huge change from the radio work I was doing earlier, and it may help explain why the show has done so well. It started with twenty-eight stations, and now more than one hundred stations broadcast the show every week.

It takes a lot more work to prepare for the kind of show I do now. I would watch the news anyway, because I am curious to know what is happening in our country and around the world, but I have to make an extra effort to catch the news at least once a day. I try to pick up a variety of papers, too. My regular papers are *USA Today,* the *New York Times,* the *Wall Street Journal,* and the *Commercial Appeal* in Tennessee, all of which I read pretty much every day. But when I am traveling around the country, I like to pick up different papers to get a feel for different regions. The most important day of the week is Sunday and not only because I do my show that day. I have to watch all the Sunday shows, like *Meet the Press,* to see what's going on and what people are talking about.

That's the main way my show has changed. I am just a lot more prepared than I used to be. If I know what has been discussed on all the other shows, then on my show I try to talk about things that have been overlooked during the week. I think that makes the show more interesting. Anybody can copy someone else. They do it all the time. But I have my two hours to fill up however I see fit, so it's up to me not to go the easy way and just follow the big events of the day or week and talk about all the same old stuff. Michael Jackson might have been discussed all week long, but I am not going to discuss him on my show unless I think I have something fresh to add.

I like to find something good and jump on it. For instance, if Ted Kennedy does something stupid, I might have some fun with that on my show. Last October, he voted the wrong way on two bills. "The Senate chamber was filled with audible gasps . . . when Sen. Edward M. Kennedy, the pro-choice champion, clearly voted 'yes' on final passage of the bill to ban partial-birth abortion," columnist Robert Novak reported. Kennedy also got confused later that same day voting on a Democrat-backed amendment that would have required Iraq to repay some U.S. aid. It was so blatant that the head of the Democrats in the Senate, Tom Daschle, had to go and ask the senator to change his vote.

So I did a nice little parody about Ted Kennedy and that segment turned into an hour and a half of the show. People loved it and kept calling in to pile on. Other than Novak, the story about Ted Kennedy embarrassing himself so badly kind of got missed, but come on. He screwed up, and there's no excuse for that. How many years has he been in the Senate? How many decades? They said the wording was confusing, but he wrote one of those bills himself. So how bad could the wording be? I'm sure if all the other senators could figure it out, Ted Kennedy probably could, too. But he was somehow the only one who had to change his vote. I like to bring attention to stories like that. I figure if a lot of people are calling in to express their outrage, they will probably be telling other people what they heard and maybe that will help kick-start some discussion of the issues.

I love that feeling. I love knowing that people are talking and expressing ideas that they might never have been expressing if they had not listened to my show. To me, radio is almost like a drug. Once you get into it, you never want to quit. I would never tell anybody who pays me the truth about this, but I would do it for free, because I love it that much. Radio gets in your blood. So I don't think I will ever leave radio, even if I end up doing more TV.

CHAPTER 3

The Importance of Family— Homeschooling

I never went to nursery school. Or kindergarten. Or elementary school. My parents did some research about homeschooling in Tennessee and decided that it made sense to try it. They met with several friends who were already engaged in homeschooling, and learned about the many positive aspects of this new educational frontier. They even lobbied for favorable homeschool legislation in our state. My mother was trained at the University of Tennessee at Martin, and she knew from her experience in the classroom at several schools just how little teaching goes on in a room packed with thirty or more children. Mostly the kids just sit around and get maybe thirty or forty minutes of real education here and there over the course of a day. My mother knew she could do a lot better than that, teaching my sister and me right there in the dining room, especially when we were young, because she had taught elementary school.

People who have never been through homeschooling would be

surprised how normal it can seem. It was what we knew. It was how we lived. My mother would take turns, teaching me for a while and then teaching my sister for a while. I was two years behind my sister, because I was younger, so she couldn't teach us the same subjects at the same time. We might both be doing English, but I would be working on phonics or whatever and my sister would be working on writing. Or we might both be doing math but each studying something different. There was no way to hide. My mother was right there, and she always knew what we were doing and whether we were really trying or just coasting a little.

It was awful, in some ways, having reading, writing, and arithmetic 24/7. I have never been a big academic guy, and my mother was all about the fundamentals. So she would drive it into us, and we really never left school with my mother. If we used a pronoun incorrectly, even if it was right in the middle of our birthday celebration, she would correct us right away. You could try to kid her, saying something like, "Gosh, Mom, school is over today." But it never worked. She was never going to give it up. In fact, she still hasn't.

"I'm the unofficial English professor in our home, and there are times when my family would like for me to resign from chairing the Ferguson School of English Grammar," my mother says. "Who else would tell Ben on a regular basis to enhance his vocabulary or that he should brush up on his objective and nominative pronoun chart? It bugs me when I am listening to him on the radio and he uses an adjective when he should have used an adverb. As I tell him often, no one else cares enough about him to tell him these things, and if your mother doesn't care enough to help you out, who will?"

My mother worked hard to keep our educations lively by giving us a lot of field trips, too. She gave us the chance to do a lot of different things. My sister took ballet when she was young, and she also went horseback riding and had piano lessons in the middle of the day. That was good, having other things that interrupted the schooling so it wouldn't feel too regimented or routine. My mother used incentives, too. My sister wanted to be free to go socialize, and I wanted to have time to go shoot baskets or practice my tennis. So my mother always set it up so that if we finished early, we could go do something we wanted to do. That really tended to sharpen our concentration and speed us through our schoolwork.

I liked homeschooling. I had more free time than other kids, and I made the most of it. Later, my sister decided to go to a private school. She started in the eleventh grade. I was busy with radio and tennis and didn't want to give any of that up. My mindset was, "Heck, no, I'm not going." I could go have tennis lessons in the middle of the day, when my coach wasn't busy, and he gave them to me for free. He took me under his wing, becoming almost a second dad. If I had been available only after normal school hours, I never would have had that opportunity. I also would not have been able to do my Thursday-afternoon radio show, which ran from three to six, if I had been in a regular school, because I always needed time to prepare beforehand.

Social life was never a problem, since I was busy with tennis, church, and other activities. People would make snide little comments, mostly to my mother about my schooling. "So when are you going to put your kids in a real school?" as if we were somehow learning less than the kids stuck in public school with overworked teachers who barely knew their names. If other parents said anything like that to me directly, I was thinking "I do exactly what your kids do, and I see them after school." I was never shy about talking with parents and debating the merits of homeschooling, and those discussions helped get me ready for going on the radio later and holding my own against people a lot older than me.

I didn't exactly cry when my sister decided to go to school, leaving my mother and me from the time I was in ninth grade. Like any brother and sister, we could get on each other's nerves, so I was kind of glad, actually when she started school. People thought it must have been overwhelming for me, spending so much time alone with my mother, but it worked out fine. I was always busy and always on the go. Also, by then she kind of pointed me in a direction and had me do my work. If I had a question, I would ask her, but it wasn't as if she turned the dining room into a lecture hall and delivered hour-long talks while I was expected to take detailed notes. She also let me set my own schedule, so a lot of times, I would come back from a radio show at six and do two hours of school because I previously had time to do only a few hours that morning before leaving.

There were plenty of skeptics. People thought it was really weird what we were doing. They assumed I must be getting a terrible education. Even relatives often had doubts about whether I was really learning very much. But I wouldn't have had it any other way. If you were in a classroom, the teacher would spend a lot of time moving around the classroom talking to other students and would give you only a little time. My mother kept busy around the house, but if I needed to ask her something, she was always available. She knew how I learned. She knew how my brain worked. She was always very good at getting a point across, usually quickly and painlessly. That was why we were so efficient with our time. Also, I could sit there and eat my lunch and study at the same time. That was great. I didn't want to go to regular school, because I knew how much time I would be wasting there.

Finally, we decided it made sense for me to go to a private school starting in the eleventh grade. My mother's teaching experience was with the lower grades, and upper-level math and higher sciences were not her strong points. I picked up some of that here and there through homeschool groups with certified teachers. I studied art and Latin that way, for example. A few of us went to the house of a Latin teacher on Tuesdays and Thursdays, and she taught us the language for two and a half hours each time. She had a child and wanted to stay at home, but she still wanted to do some teaching, so it worked out well for everyone. I studied chemistry during my tenth-grade year with a high-school chemistry teacher who wanted to make a little extra money on the side.

My last two years of high school, I went part-time to a small private school in Memphis called Westminster Academy. I took three classes in the morning and then left in the afternoon so I could play tennis. I also started on the Westminster varsity basketball team my junior and senior years, and we won our conference my last year there. Westminster was a good chance for me to get more grounding in the classics, studying Aristotle and other literature. I had some catching up to do, especially in math. I had to take algebra my eleventh-grade year. That felt kind of weird, sitting there with all those eighth-graders, but I didn't feel stupid or anything. I just took the class to catch up. If anybody tried to make fun of me, I didn't really care, because I knew that I had experienced things others only dreamed of doing. Plus I already had a college scholarship waiting for me.

I was looking forward to college. A lot of people kept saying I was going to fail completely when I hit college. Even my mother worried a lot. She fretted that she had not prepared me well enough. But I wasn't freaking out about that at all. I knew I would do fine. I ended up carrying a 3.0 grade-point average in college, taking as many as twenty-one hours some semesters. A 3.0 for playing college tennis, writing this book, and doing my radio show, plus TV, I figure is not too bad.

If I had it all to do over, I would definitely want to be homeschooled again. Back when I was in homeschool, it was a time when people were a little touchy and insecure, and they had bumper stickers saying things like HOMESCHOOLERS HAVE CLASS. It used to be quite controversial. Now most people do not see it as abnormal, I think, and that is a good thing.

I admit, there were days when I got a little tired of spending so much time with my mother. I love her to death, and we will always be close, but sometimes she bothers me. That's no surprise, considering all that time we spent together. I just have a shorter fuse with her. I wouldn't call it a temper, but sometimes I just have less patience with her. I am probably closer to my father now as a result. But my mother was a huge influence on me through homeschooling. She molded me into the man I am now. She was always telling me I had to have discipline and be as honest as the day is long. She harped on standing up for what you believe in, especially on moral issues.

I am not sure homeschooling is the answer for everyone. It really depends on the circumstances. My parents encouraged extracurricular activities. They didn't care what we did—piano or baseball or soccer—just so long as we were exposed to a variety of experiences and took part in group activities with other kids. Church activities took on a higher importance, too, and I remember I would always look forward to Wednesday night youth group. I think my parents did a good job of keeping my sister and me grounded in reality. They understood that there are bad things in the world, but you have to let a kid be normal.

Some kids who do homeschooling really suffer because they don't have any social interaction with other students, and that makes them awkward and nervous around other people. That's really sad. They end up being antisocial. Some parents try to use homeschooling to shelter their children from the evils of the world, which sounds good in concept but just isn't reality. You can't do that. You can't use homeschooling to pull kids out of society, and if that is why you are doing it, then I think you are homeschooling for the wrong reason.

If you're homeschooling because you think you can give your kids a better education, then I would say, yes, do it. Unfortunately, however, I know kids who were homeschooled and it totally messed them up. Their parents used homeschooling almost like a jail to keep them apart from society, imprisoning them in a little bubble. They have seriously brainwashed their children into being freaks with no social skills whatsoever.

Most likely, I plan to have my own children homeschooled at least for first, second, and third grades. That is when it has the most benefit and when you can really establish a foundation of learning in the basic skills of education, reading, writing, and arithmetic. Later on I would probably leave it up to the kids. I never begged or cried to go to school. When my sister said she was ready to go, my parents sent her to a private school. I would defiantly put my kids in homeschooling if I thought it was the best situation at the time, but I would have no problem sending them to school either.

I haven't tried to encourage others to use homeschooling, because too often I've seen it used for the wrong reasons. I've seen it abused. So usually when somebody tells me, "I want to homeschool my kids," I ask them some tough questions. What are your reasons for wanting to homeschool? Do you believe you are going to turn your kid into some kind of instant superstar? I have run into a lot of psycho parents, as I call them, who are overly protective and overly involved. Those are the last people on earth who should be homeschooling.

The people who really give homeschooling a bad name are parents who are just terrified of the world and terrified that their kids are going to get pregnant or get on drugs, so they take an attitude of "We will just shelter them from anything and everything and never let them see any of the real world." In reality that just ensures that the kids are going to turn out screwed-up. They are going to try so hard in their twenties to experience that which they were sheltered from. I know. I've seen this happen. The people who use homeschooling for the wrong reasons give their kids no chance to ever make anything of themselves, and that is when it's wrong.

I'll be the first to tell you there are some weird people who homeschool their kids. Some of the weirdest people I've met are homeschoolers, in fact. Some are just not normal. I'd even call some of them creepy. They can't relate at all to normal Americans. Some of them are conspiracy-theory types. I knew homeschoolers who really, truly believed that in the year 2000 at twelve oh-one on January 1, the whole world was going to end. A lot of extremists homeschool because they think the whole world is against them. So they victimize their children by making them paranoid and saying, "You're not going to school! Awful things happen there." That is when it's not fair, and I feel really sorry for their kids.

CHAPTER 4

The Importance of Family— My Parents

My father's side of the family spent several generations farming big stretches of land in North Dakota. Carrots, raspberries, wheat—they farmed it all, they had so much land up there. The name Ferguson is Scottish, but my father's family moved to this country generations ago. My father was the oldest of four, and he moved with his family to Memphis when he was in the fifth grade because his father was a lumber salesman for Weyerhaeuser and that was where they sent him.

My father's mother died of cancer when he was eighteen years old. That was hard on him, especially as the oldest of four, and I think that loss shaped him to be the way he is. He's a very patient man and very, very understanding. He kind of had to take care of his family because he was the oldest, he had three younger siblings to look after, and his father was a traveling salesman.

My father went to elementary school and high school in Memphis and graduated from the University of Memphis with a degree in criminal justice. He always wanted to go into law enforcement. He always liked to help people. That was his knack, helping people. He was a policeman in a Memphis suburb called Germantown for two years and then went to work as an I.C.C. railroad detective, working a lot of night shifts. I remember going to work with him, and it was really fun. He was driving a big Dodge Ramcharger with the blue lights. That was really cool.

He brought me along only when he had a partner working with him. They would get a call and would hurry over somewhere to check out people breaking into boxcars. He took me along so that I could get a sense of what his job was like, but I don't know how he did it. Sometimes he would be walking through the middle of a railroad yard with no lights on at all. It would be pitch-black, so you couldn't even see your hand in front of your face, and he would be all alone out there. You couldn't pay me enough to do that kind of job. No way.

He never had to shoot anybody. He got close one night. A guy kept approaching him, and my dad drew his gun and put it higher and higher. That was enough for the guy. He put his hands out, and my father didn't have to shoot him. Later, he found out the guy had brass knuckles in his pockets for both hands, so if he had gotten close enough, he probably would have shot to take my dad out.

He was laid off from that job, and after that, he wanted to join the FBI, because he thought that would take it to the next level. But he thought it over and decided family was more important than a job. He knew that if he took a job with the FBI, he would have to move to a major city, like Chicago or Dallas or New York, and he knew he didn't want to uproot his family. That was the hard part of making family life such a high priority. He pretty much conceded his dreams to fatherhood. He sold power tools for Makita for ten years, and now he works as a salesman for ITW Paslode, which makes nail guns.

He put a lot of time into being a dad. He was a terrible athlete with no knack for sports, but he was always out there coaching. Looking back, I don't think he ever liked it much, but he was one of the coaches for coach-pitch baseball, for T-ball, for everything. We would play catch, too, even though he never looked very comfortable throwing or catching a baseball. He would shoot basketball with me, too. I loved it so much I would stand out there all afternoon, just shooting again and again and again, so much that I actually broke the metal on the back of the rim. I just literally wore it out from hitting it so many times with the ball. We would play H-O-R-S-E for hours, even though I usually won, and he took me to all my games, too. He was never one to talk strategy before a game. I was on my own with that side of things. But he was definitely supportive. I played on basketball teams every year when I was young, until kids started getting old enough to play for their school teams instead of for community centers or the church league. Because I was homeschooled, that was the end of the run until I went to Westminster and got to play again.

My father is probably the most patient man I've met in my entire life, and I think the older I've gotten, the more I've tried to look to him as an example. That's not always easy. Sometimes his patience is really frustrating. Like, how can you be so patient? He's extremely good at his job, for example, but he's been there for too long. It frustrates me to see that, but he's content with his life and loyal to his company, so what can I say?

He's also very calm. He never yells. (Well, okay, sometimes he has to yell at me.) I learned from him to keep work life and personal life separate. He was always able to keep the stress of being a police officer or a railroad detective completely separate from his home life. He had to deal with extreme stress, but I never remember seeing him in a bad mood after work. He could leave it at the door, and I feel that's probably one of the biggest things I've learned from him. For instance if I'm on TV and you and I are debating, I'm going to go at you 110 percent, and I hope I kick your rear end. It's not personal, though. We could go to dinner afterward and put the debate behind us. I think you have to do that. You can see where politics distorts people. They can't separate politics from their personal life and don't know any more who they are as a person.

Sometimes the lessons my dad taught me about patience were hard to take. I was always so eager to get to the next level. I never liked sitting at the kids' table for Christmas and Thanksgiving. The adults' table intrigued me. Not that I was an abnormal kid. I played with GI Joe and made fun of girls for playing with Barbies. But I was around kids all the time, so during the holidays I wanted to hang out with the adults to see what they talked about. My father understood how much I wanted to be at the other table, but he always told me to be patient.

"Patience is a virtue, Ben," he would tell me. "Your time will come. Trust me: Enjoy it while you can."

I wasn't ready to hear that, but it made an impression anyway. A lot of people say if you are young and you have some success, you are going to be arrogant and cocky. A lot of people wanted to label me that way, and they wanted to see me fail. My father has been really good about keeping me grounded and humble. If I am out of line, he lets me know it. Many times he has sat me down and said, "You need to watch yourself, son, you need to be a little more respectful." Sometimes that happened when adults would belittle me because of my age. That really ticked me off. My father would tell me, "Look, don't worry about them. Hold on to your dignity."

He always had zero tolerance for anyone showing a lack of respect to anyone else. All the big conversations we had were about respect. That was how I would get into trouble with him. He laid down the law, and that was it. The issue was settled. He always had his eye out, ready to tell me when I needed to watch myself. That week I spent in Washington when I was thirteen years old, doing my first radio show, was a real thrill for me, and I remember him talking to me on the flight home to Tennessee and telling me, "It's going to be a little different for a while when you get home. Be yourself, say thank you, and I probably wouldn't talk about the strip too much."

That was his way of protecting me and making sure I didn't get a big head. The Associated Press ran a story. I was in the Memphis paper three times in barely two weeks, and the TV stations did spots on my coming back home after the week in D.C. was over. My dad did a really good job of reminding me that I was still a person just like anyone else, and what you do should not define who you are. That's why I think now it's been so much fun doing what I'm doing. I don't feel any pressure to succeed. I don't think I have to prove anything. I don't think I have to get anybody's respect.

I had a hard time when I was younger. I wanted to win every argument, and I mean *every single* argument. Winning was everything to me. Sometimes I would even lie to win an argument. My biggest asset and my biggest weakness when I was younger was that I could manipulate people pretty well. My father knew that about me, and he watched me closely. He wanted to break that habit as quickly as possible and get me to cut it out. Call it what you want, but lying is lying. I remember a couple of times when I used radio as an excuse. When I started going to Latin and chemistry classes with real teachers, I would say something like, "You know, I'm sorry I don't have my homework in today, but I was doing my radio show yesterday."

The truth was, I could have gotten the homework done. It was just an excuse. My father found out I had used radio that way, and he made himself very clear to me. "If you're going to use your show as an excuse again, that's it, we'll take you off the radio," he said. I got the message, too. He was right. I could have done the homework. I just got lazy. And I knew I could use a half truth about radio to get another day to do the work.

Or I would be having a discussion with my mom and always wanting to have the last word, and I would manipulate what happened a little. I found out that worked really well. But my father would see right through me. He would say, "That's it, no more." I was on the phone one day trying to book a guest for my show, and later I said that was why I didn't get my work done. My father said, "Well then, fine, we'll just get rid of the radio." He was calling my bluff. Teachers and my mother may have been more understanding, but he was saying, "Uh-huh, uh-huh, here's your professional work and here's your schoolwork, so you separate them, or I'll separate them for you." There was no BS.

When I think of my father I think of a man who supports what I do. He likes politics but does not love it like I do. None the less he talks about it with me. He does not love sports like I do, but he still worked with me and supported me to become a better athlete. He spent countless hours going over schoolwork with me, and I know he didn't enjoy doing it, but he did it for me. He knew what made me tick and he made sure he was a part of it.

To this day, I don't think either my father or my mother can actually tell you how to keep score in tennis. I kid you not. They just don't know. Which is kind of embarrassing, but it's great, too, because they didn't care if I won or lost as long as I enjoyed it and loved the game. They saw other parents push their kids too hard and make them burn out, and they never wanted me to go through that.

My mother is from Little Rock, Arkansas, home of Bill Clinton, and, like a lot of people from that part of the country, she is very talkative and very emotional. She is not one to back down. She never wants to do something before she is good and ready to do it. Just ask my father. They met through a friend in a Bible study group in Memphis after she had graduated from college. He asked her to marry him after they had been dating one and a half years.

"I'll think about it," she told him.

Two and a half weeks later, she still hadn't answered him.

"All right, give me an answer," he finally had to tell her.

She finally said "Yes".

She explained later that it was an important decision, and she did not want to make a mistake. She is the kind of person who needs time to make a good decision. But come on! If I asked somebody to marry me and two weeks later she was still thinking about it, I would tell her, "Never mind, that must be a warning sign. I'm done. Have a great life." But that is how my mother is. She takes her time, no matter what anyone says.

It was the same way when I was born. Two days went by, and I still had no name. My mother kept saying she needed more time to decide on a name. My father was going crazy. They'd had nine months to think about it! He finally called her from work one day to get her to make a choice.

He told her, "Everybody has asked me the name of my son, and I can't tell them because I don't know myself. We're naming him today."

My mother would ask herself, "Is he a Todd? Is he a Matt? Is he a Benjamin?" Once my father said it was time to decide, they finalized it with Benjamin Grant Ferguson.

Like my dad, my mom is always keeping after me to make sure I don't let my success with radio go to my head. She always says she is my biggest critic, and it's true, too. She might give me a call after a show or a TV appearance and instead of telling me how wonderful it was, she will ask, "Well, how did you think it went?" Translated, that basically means "You sucked!" She would never admit that, but I know it's true. She's kind of a worrywart. I don't worry about anything. If something bad happens, fine, I just try to roll with it and move on to the next thing. But my mother will talk about it for a week. We're totally different that way.

She has taught me a lot about persistence. She is without a doubt the most persistent person I have ever met in my life. It's unreal. She loves to say, "I've told you that five thousand times, Benjamin!" and it is not as much of an exaggeration as you might think. I always think she will eventually give up on something, but she never does. She will always come up to me and kind of comb my hair to the side with her hand and tell me, "If you do that every day, it will train it to stay there on its own."

And I tell her, "Mom, I'm twenty-two now, and it's not going to happen so please just give it up."

I think some of that persistence transferred to me, and it has really helped me. I can't tell you how many times different people have told me I couldn't do something, and I ignored them and went right on and did what I set out to do. Dozens and dozens of people told me it would never, ever happen that I would be asked at age seventeen or nineteen or twenty-two to come on Fox or CNN as a commentator, and if I had listened to them, I never would be where I am now. But my mother taught me to grin and say thank you and just ignore what people say and stay on the track you set for yourself. She has taught me that we all need to be who we are and not to try to be someone else.

She also taught me never to be afraid to admit mistakes. That's part of growing up and learning, because if you never admit that you're wrong, you're never going to grow up. I don't think any of us has ever met someone who is right all the time. But that takes time to learn. If I was wrong, my mother would push me to admit I was wrong, and I fought that kicking and screaming the whole way. I would be saying, "No, I am not wrong!" I really didn't think I was. But she was persistent and eventually she would wear me down and I would say, "Okay, fine, I was wrong." Sometimes that took days. Other times I refused to admit I was wrong even though I knew I was.

"Well, I just don't think we see eye to eye," I would say.

I would be trying to twist or manipulate the situation. My mother wouldn't let me get away with it.

"You're wrong," she would keep repeating.

She would wear me out.

"Okay, fine, will you just leave me alone if I admit I was wrong?" I would say eventually.

My mother pays a lot of attention to distant family members, family heritage, family tree, and family history. Being together on the holidays is a huge priority for her. I think my dad recognized that, and that is why we never moved from Memphis. It was worth the sacrifice to him. I'm different. There is no way I could marry somebody if I knew I would always have to live in one place.

My mother's mother died when I was ten. My grandmother and I were very close, and I remember her well. I cried at her funeral, and not because you are supposed to cry, but because I truly missed her that much. I just wish she could have seen me on TV one time or heard me on the radio. I think she would have been proud. I'm not an emotional person, but that is one wish I have. She taught me so much when I was younger, not only bits of knowledge but also about priorities.

She always talked to me about honesty. That was her top priority. I think she had seen a lot of men ruin their lives by not being honest, especially in politics, where so much power and money are involved. I think honesty is the first thing that goes with most people. People are good at manipulating the truth. They are good at using their rhetorical skills to get out of things and to win even when they should lose. I think my grandmother probably saw some of that in me. She saw I was good with words and a real talker, and I think she recognized that could be my downfall. Probably she saw some of the characteristics of my personality and knew I could use them for good or bad.

I am lucky, I know, to have had strong influences like my parents and my grandmother to help pound some hard lessons into my head, especially on the topic of honesty. I could have made some different choices and taken different positions on my radio show. I could have said what the Republicans wanted me to say. But I speak my mind and go to bed at night knowing that I told the truth. I used my show to call on Trent Lott to resign, which was probably the worst political move I could ever make. But it felt right to me, and I would do the same thing again tomorrow. I like ticking people off, and if you can tick somebody off and know you're doing the right thing, too, that's like winning twice.

Family reunions can be a real adventure for me. Since my mother's side of the family comes from Arkansas, a lot of my relatives are Democrats and liberals who love Bill Clinton. One of my cousins is the head of the Arkansas Democratic House Caucus. Another of my cousins, Eddie Powell, was mayor of North Little Rock from 1974 to 1979, so most political heritage I have from my family is liberal. They would always have a great time antagonizing me any chance they got. I was always the target. It drove them crazy that I'm in their family. They would say, "Send him to Arkansas for a month and we'll fix him." They've been saying that since I was thirteen years old. I just might have to take them up on the offer one of these days and drop in for a visit. They wouldn't change my mind, but maybe I would change theirs on a few subjects. Actually, I might not have to bother. I put in a call to my cousin Eddie Powell not long ago, just to kid him about liberal politics. Turns out he has changed with the times. "I didn't leave the Democrat Party, the Democratic Party left me," he told me. I guess it really is true that we get wiser with age.

CHAPTER 5

Always Up to Something

I was always hustling to do something to earn some spending money. I've never had a job working for minimum wage, but I have always found other ways to make a buck. Some of the stuff I came up with is pretty funny. I bought a tennis stringer at one point, and I would string rackets like crazy. I got pretty good at it. I would stay up late, watching TV and doing my work, and I got really fast. I could do three rackets in an hour, so that worked out to fifteen dollars an hour. That is a lot better than what they would have paid me to work the counter at McDonald's or Starbucks. That wasn't for me. I never wanted to have a boss, and in a sense I never really have.

I bought stock by myself when I was about ten years old. I was reading the *Wall Street Journal* and talking stocks with adults in the neighborhood, so I thought I knew what I was doing. Plus, I had a little money I had saved from my own lawn business. I started that when I was nine. I called it You Grow It, We Mow It, and I would walk around the neighborhood with the family push mower and do as many lawns as possible. If you have ever mowed a lawn with a push mower, you know it is definitely work, not like unleashing one of those expensive power mowers that will gobble up a small dog in no time if you don't keep close watch. People in the South have big lawns, so that was a lot of mowing. I started out by walking across the street to ask the neighbor if he wanted his lawn cut, and that neighbor said yes. Then I went next door and then down the street. I made ten or fifteen bucks per yard. Later I recruited a friend in the neighborhood who would cut lawns for me. I paid him seven bucks a lawn and pocketed the rest.

I was always looking for a new angle. Like kids everywhere, we would get into shaving-cream fights sometimes, especially if we went on a church trip. I noticed that there never seemed to be enough shaving cream. Kids would always run out. So I thought ahead and made a mental note to myself to load up on shaving cream for the next trip. I went to Wal-Mart and stocked up on the cheapest shaving cream I could find, Barbasol, which only cost ninety-seven cents a can. I sold all those cans and wound up with forty bucks in profit. It was highway robbery, but hey, they were willing to pay it. I had some explaining to do when I got home after that.

"Where did you get this money?" my parents asked me.

"I sold shaving cream for five bucks a can," I told them.

My main motivation with the lawn business and other moneymaking ideas was basketball. I was a huge fan of the University of Memphis basketball team, and I decided I just had to have season tickets. Memphis basketball was all that mattered to me. There was no professional basketball team I cared about, so all my attention was focused on college hoops. I would do anything I could to go to the games from the time I was six years old. My mother enjoyed Memphis basketball, and her enthusiasm rubbed off on me from an early age. Different people would take me to games—a neighbor, the family doctor, other family friends, my parents. It was always one parent or the other. They would trade off. They knew how important it was for me to see every game.

We all went crazy in 1992 when the U of M team had such a great run in the NCAA tournament. That was the first year that Anfernee Hardaway and David Vaughn played together, and the Tigers had an amazing run. They won ten of their last thirteen regular-season games, squeaked into the tournament as a sixth seed in the Midwest Regional, and then beat Pepperdine and Arkansas to send them into the Sweet Sixteen. We had a Sweet Sixteen party at our house, with neighbors and other friends, and I just loved every minute of it. Billy Smith hit that one-hander with eleven seconds left against Georgia Tech to send the game into overtime, and then Memphis won it, and they were one of eight teams left in the tournament. They lost their next game, but what a thrill it was in our house.

I knew all the players and their numbers. My favorite was Elliott Perry, who had the big goggles and wore his socks pulled up so high, they were almost up to his knees. He graduated in 1991 as Memphis's all-time leading scorer; later he had his number retired, and he went on to a pretty solid NBA career. I also remember this guy named John McLaughlin who never made it. He was a point guard, and one thing he could do was shoot three-pointers. The main time he got to play was at the end of the game, when Memphis was behind, and they would send him out there to try to hit a three. He was another favorite of mine, because I was always the big guy who wanted to shoot three-pointers.

I was a center, because I was tall, but I always wanted to shoot threes. It was really kind of funny, because the first time I played in a real full-court game, I never got a chance to take any outside shots because I was a center and would just get a rebound and put it back up. Then in the second half the opposing team tried a half-court press against us, and a teammate passed the ball to me around midcourt. That was my chance!

I heaved it from just inside the half-court line and swished it. It should have been a three-pointer, but this was a church league game, and they didn't even have a three-point line.

I play a little golf. I love golf, but tennis became my sport. I fell into it when I was twelve or thirteen. An aunt of mine lived in Alaska, and she played a lot of racquetball up there, since you can play even in the depths of winter. She used to give me racquetball rackets for Christmas, and I would go to the country club and play racquetball by myself because there was no one around who wanted to play. The tennis pro at the club felt sorry for me.

"Why don't you play tennis?" he asked me one day. "There are actually other kids to play with."

So I tried tennis. A neighbor had played college tennis for the University of Memphis, and he taught me how to play. I would go with his kids to Colonial Country Club, which is where President Ford hit a hole in one when he was president. We weren't members, but our neighbors were. I was kind of a hitting partner for the neighbors' kids, since I was a little older and could hit a little harder. Their dad figured that was good practice for his kids.

I got more and more into playing, and my game improved. The tennis coach at Colonial gave my parents a discount to get me into some clinics. His name was Mark Bran, and he liked having me around because I was a little better than the kids he was teaching. He says that he liked teaching me because I was eager to learn and listened to everything he said. Either way, it was a trade-off. I would cut his lawn in exchange for tennis lessons. My parents would drive me over to his house on Saturdays and I would cut his lawn, and then they would drive me over to the country club and he would give me a lesson. This was when I was thirteen. Lessons were fifty dollars an hour, and my parents couldn't afford that. I pretty much did what I had to do and I loved it. So I started playing and never quit.

I really wanted to run for office when I was younger. It became a big thing on my radio show. People made mugs and T-shirts saying "Ben Ferguson for President 2020." I did the math and it worked out that I would be thirty-five by then so I would be old enough to run for President. My slogan was "Ben Ferguson for President 2020, Perfect Vision for the Future." A lot of listeners got involved. One guy who had a banner business heard my radio show and sent me banners reading BEN FERGUSON FOR PRESIDENT 2020. I put those up. I was serious. I really wanted to be president, and I didn't care if people told me, "Oh, you're crazy! That's impossible."

But I've lost some of that drive. The more I learn about both parties, the less I want to run for any office at any level. If the timing was right and I thought I could truly make a difference, more so than on radio or TV, then yeah, I would do it. Or if there was a politician I thought was a complete crook, and I could run against him, I might do that. It would have to be something personal that would get me to do it.

I would like to teach at some point, just to show that you don't have to be an Ivy League type to teach at the college level. I have had some bad experiences with teachers who went out of their way to discourage me without even knowing what they were talking about. I had one teacher my freshman year at Tusculum College in Greenville, Tennessee, who was in the journalism department. I didn't tell him anything about my background or all the work I had done in radio or how many times I had been on national television already at that age. He met with me for five or ten minutes, gave me kind of a funny look, and said, "Ben, I really don't think you have the knack for radio and TV."

That could have really slowed me down. It could have ruined my entire career. I just thanked him for his thoughts and left, and then the next day I slid a videotape and a cassette under his door. The video showed me on CNN and MSNBC, and the cassette had a recording of one of my radio shows. So what do you think he said after that? What do you think he did? Nothing. Nothing at all. He was probably too embarrassed, but that's no excuse. Too many people who end up teaching are people like him. To me that guy was the classic example of someone who never made it, so instead he taught. He talked down to his students as if we were all stupid, when obviously he didn't know the first thing about what it takes to succeed in radio and TV.

I don't know what his problem was or why he treated me the way he did. I think some professors graded me a little tougher because they knew who I was and what I was doing. I don't know if it was jealousy, but there were times when teachers would try to belittle me in front of other students. I think they were thinking, Why in the heck should this guy get to have a nationally syndicated radio show? It's often just a total negative, instead of "We're proud, we're excited for you," and that kind of thing.

Those bad experiences have made me want to teach even more. I'd like to teach political science and journalism and sit around and talk about politics and the media. I'd love to teach at a liberal university. I would much rather teach people who disagree with me than teach people who agree with me. I could be a good example, I think, because there are a lot of kids who are never going to be 4.0 types but who are still bright and still have something to offer. Maybe I could encourage them. I struggled to maintain a B average, but I always had my hands on things. I had my hands on radio. I had my hands on TV. I had my hands in tennis. So when you have all those things going on, grades aren't the number-one priority.

CHAPTER 6

Adventures in Radio and Television

I have great respect for certain people whom I disagree with completely. I have tons of respect for James Carville, for example. I wouldn't agree with him on the color of the sky, but he's good at what he does. I would probably rate him the best guest I've ever had on my show, even though he's a liberal. Carville came on my show when I was seventeen, and he showed me the respect to argue like crazy. I like that. I respect the heck out of that. He is passionate and well informed, and he likes to roll up his sleeves and sling it around. I never have a problem with somebody totally disagreeing with me unless he tries to make it personal and starts calling me an idiot or making blanket statements about "you people on the right" or "you conservatives" or "you Republicans" or "you talk-show hosts." Carville isn't that way at all. He has done his homework, and he always has facts ready to back up what he says. I am sure he and I will get more chances to go at it, maybe while I am out promoting this book, so keep your eyes open. I can promise you it will be a colorful battle.

Dick Morris has to be the worst guest I ever had on the show. It is truly amazing that the man has had as much success as he has. He is just plain dull. Every sentence out of his mouth was boring, boring, boring. I've never heard so many umms, ahhs, and uhhs in my life. I had to cut the segment short to get him off the air; that's how bad he was. I am sure he is a bright guy, but he is one of those backroom types who feels more comfortable when he can scheme and strategize in private and take all the time he needs. He freezes up under pressure. That is why he was an adviser and not a leader. He was going through a tough time when I had him on the show. He had just been busted for telling secrets to a prostitute, but I didn't ask him about that at all. We were just talking politics in general. I was ready for this amazingly brilliant, quick-witted character, but it just wasn't there. That interview was a real nightmare. It just goes to show that big reputations don't always add up.

One of my most memorable experiences was my first appearance on national television. I had been on local TV in Tennessee a few times, starting when I was thirteen, and I was getting attention for my first radio show. The first time I went on national TV was when Bill O'Reilly had me on his show to talk about the youth vote in the 2000 primaries. I guess you could call that my coming-out party. I was only seventeen at the time, and it was just Bill and me, one on one. I was pretty nervous, too. You're sitting there in the chair under the hot lights and they keep teasing your segment, building up the anticipation. Your heart really starts to pound the first time you go through something like that.

That was a tough introduction to big-time TV. I studied up for more than two days and was ready with a lot of facts and figures kicking around in my head. I had been going over my arguments about youth voting, and I really felt good. But there was one small problem. Bill had changed his mind about what he wanted to talk about, but no one tipped me off. So there I was, totally on a different wavelength than he was. He started bombarding me with questions about every candidate in the Republican primary. I was not ready to talk about Alan Keys or Bob Dornan or any of the other lesser candidates in the race. It was tough going. And Bill kept interrupting me and cutting me off. It was a real trial by fire. I thought I held my own, though, even when he made it hard on me.

"So do your friends think you're a geek?" he asked me.

I said no, but he continued to badger me about not being a normal seventeen-year-old. He asked me for details on the latest installments of *Buffy the Vampire Slayer,* as if that was some cool show or something, which it wasn't. He kept asking about whether I talked politics with my friends, even after I told him I didn't. I laughed it all off. I thought it was funny he was trying so hard to make me look like a dork.

I learned a real lesson that day. It's fine to be excited about going on national TV. That just shows you are human. But you can never assume you know just what to expect. The medium doesn't work that way. It is way too unpredictable. So if you are going to be on live TV, you better have something to say on every subject imaginable, because you never know when a host will try to catch you off guard by changing the subject on you. Also: Do research about the show that has asked you to be a guest. I had never seen Bill O'Reilly's show before I was a guest. Fox was still a smaller network at that time, and we did not get it on Memphis cable. I figured that the show was like all the other shows I had seen, that I could expect a straightforward Q-and-A session with a nice little warm-up and all that. If I had known more about the show, I would have expected to feel as if I was being thrown into the deep end of the pool when I don't even know how to swim. That is what it feels like to be on Bill's show when you don't know what he is like.

I guess I had the last laugh, though. I figure I can handle just about any challenge on TV now. Compared to the experience of going on with Bill when he was trying to make me look like a dork and a geek and cutting me off every chance he got, everything else seems pretty easy. The funny thing was, one of *The O'Reilly Factor* producers later sent me a bunch of e-mails from viewers talking about what a great guest I had been. Some of them said they wanted to see me back on the show as a regular election commentator. Some said that Bill should watch his back because I looked as if I was ready to take his job from him. Some said I should run for president. And, yes, some others said I was pathetic.

That gave me some confidence. Now I actually like it when I go on TV and they change the topic at the last minute. I figure that's a good way to see who really has something to say and who is up there like a windup doll, ready to spew out whatever sound bites they studied up on that morning at home. I really love to debate on TV. I like that feeling of going at it with someone and having a good fight over ideas, and I always try to remind myself to have fun and never to take myself too seriously.

I would say the most fun I ever had on a single TV appearance was on another Fox News show, *Dayside with Linda Vester,* when I went up against Ellen Ratner, a Fox News analyst and radio commentator. That was a blast because I just blew her out of the water. The audience applauded for me at least ten times and not a single time for her. She figured it would be a piece of cake for someone like her who studied at Harvard to go up against me, some young guy with a face like Dennis the Menace. But she paid a price on national TV for underestimating me. I just killed her, and the audience was totally on my side, even though she is paid by Fox to do what she does and I was there as a guest. The next time we debate, maybe she will do her homework a little better. And Ellen, I'm ready for a rematch, any time and anywhere. You know where to find me. I can't wait.

My next goal is to have a regular presence on TV before too long. I would love to be part of a round-table discussion every night or to have my own show. I could see myself on a show like *Politically Incorrect,* where you present a fresh report and then have a panel discussion for twenty minutes or so, featuring people with different enough perspectives to generate a lot of sparks and maybe one or two memorable one-liners. TV is great for that, because people can watch your faces and follow the argument in a way that's pretty hard on radio if you have five or six different voices overlapping all the time.

Radio is my first love, and I don't ever plan to give it up. I think for the most part it's great that radio has become more entertaining, and I think you will see that trend continue. It used to be that if you had a well-known cause, you could have a presence on radio. Now it has become a lot more simple: If you don't have ratings, you are fired. So now you have to be entertaining, and I mean entertaining all the time, no matter how amazing a command of the issues you might have. The job is not to impress people. The job is to make people want to listen to you. So often, I will hear someone on the radio who really knows a lot but just doesn't have a feel for getting that across. You almost have to feel sorry for them, because you hear their show and you just know they are not going to make it because they're not entertaining enough. My philosophy is that you have to start with being entertaining, and then you can add in your personal beliefs. If you are just an idea man, with no sense of humor and no knack for entertainment, then you're dead in the water.

Business is business at some level. Program directors look at the bottom line. If you can pull in the ratings and have the revenue coming in, then program directors don't care what you talk about. That is how Rush Limbaugh single-handedly saved AM radio. He showed that you could know a lot, you could keep up on the very latest developments on key issues, and you could have a large philosophy about the role of the United States in the world—but none of that matters if you do not start by knowing how to keep your show entertaining.

You have to learn a little perspective. You might be very passionate on a given issue, like abortion or the war on terrorism, but if you discuss that issue three hours a day every day, all week long, and keep that up for a few weeks, you are going to have about four listeners left out there, and probably all of them will be relatives tuning in so you don't hate them. You have to mix it up. You have to have a lot of variety. Not every issue you're going to talk about on the radio can be a ten on the scale of importance, and if you are always playing everything up like it is, then you are heading for trouble. I was guilty of this myself at times. Luckily, I have had people tell me I had to watch out for that. That was good advice. Sometimes you need to throw in something that is more like a two or a three in importance and make fun of it a little, and then maybe move on to something that is a six or a seven and explore that for a while. Some days, let's face it, there isn't *anything* going on that is a ten in importance, and your audience knows that.

Listeners are harder and harder to entertain, given all the options they have on radio and TV, so to survive it helps to reinvent yourself from time to time. If you can't reinvent yourself, or at least develop a new emphasis or new style, you might find yourself falling by the wayside. I have seen this happen to so many people whom I have looked up to for years, and it is painful to watch, but some were just not able to reinvent themselves and change with the times.

You have to show other sides of yourself. So in my case, there was a time when I liked being known as the youngest syndicated-radio talk-show host in the country. That got me in the door. It got me on a lot of TV shows. But now I am trying to move beyond that. The promos for my radio show do not say anything about my age. I want people to listen to me and respect me for my ideas, not because it's some kind of stunt for someone my age to be discussing the issues. I don't want it to be, "Oh, how cute, he's twenty-two years old." I want it to be, "Man, I thought he was wrong on that issue, but he makes a lot of sense, and I am going to have to look into what he said. I think he might be right." The worst possible thing I could do would be to try to hold on for too long to my old image as a kid. Just think how pathetic it would be if I were twenty-five, twenty-six, and still selling myself as superyoung. That almost discredits my ideas. Now I even ask producers not to mention my age when I go on TV. I just want to be Ben Ferguson, not the youngest this or the youngest that.

I am looking forward to watching how radio continues to change and evolve in the years ahead. I think we are going to see a lot more shows built around a specific gimmick or theme, whether it be the Idiot of the Day, the Top-Ten List of the Day, or the Political Play of the Day. People like that kind of thing. It helps them know what to expect. There will be a lot more segment-oriented radio, where the first half hour might be all about the top five candidates for Moron of the Day, and the second half hour might be something totally different. It worked for David Letterman with his opening monologue, Top-Ten List, Stupid Pet Tricks, and Stupid Human Tricks, and all of that is even before you get to the guests or the musical performance. I think you will see radio moving in that direction, too.

You will see a lot more use of bumpers, too. Bumpers are things like funny little jingles that you use to introduce a segment. You don't just have an Idiot of the Day, you have an Idiot of the Day theme song or jingle or bit that you play, and then everyone knows what they are about to hear. You turn it almost into an event. You build a little expectation. Just calling someone an idiot is no fun, but if you set it all up with a little style, a little sense of fun. then people really get a kick out of that, and they will want to hear the same segment again. They will listen for it, or you hope they will anyway.

The fact is, callers are overused on radio. Too many radio talk-show hosts use them as a crutch. They figure all they have to do is say something flamboyant and outrageous, and then the phone lines will be jammed, and they will be able to say they are having a successful show. These are the types of host who get really nervous if the phone lines aren't full. But phone calls are only a small part of a show. Success comes from connecting with a large audience, not with getting a tiny percentage of your listeners to call in. Less than 1 percent of your audience ever calls in, so you can't obsess over what the calls tell you about your show. I don't even give out my phone number the first fifteen minutes of my show. I know there is plenty of time for people to call once I have done my monologue, and if it's a little slow at first, no problem, I can just continue my monologue or start a new one. If you are really on a roll, then maybe you have your listeners mesmerized and the last thing in the world they want is to stop listening to you long enough to call up and sit there on hold waiting to talk to you directly. They should already feel they are involved in the conversation without having to call.

PART II

Telling It Like It Is

CHAPTER 7

Gun Control Means Hitting Your Target

I grew up in the Columbine era, and like anyone my age, I am tired of hearing people try to use young people as pawns in their crusade against our constitutionally protected right to bear arms. It makes me sick. I remember April 20, 1999, like it was yesterday, because I was in high school then, too, and what happened at Columbine High School felt to me and everyone my age as if it could just as easily have happened to us. It really scared us. But the twelve students and one teacher who died that day were victims of Eric Harris and Dylan Klebold, not victims of guns. The twenty other people wounded that day were victims of Eric and Dylan, not victims of guns. Gun-control nuts like to use scare tactics to sell their agenda, but the facts on gun control show how ridiculous it is to use horrendous crimes like Columbine to paint a false picture.

Gun ownership in America is at an all-time high right now, so if you believe the arguments of the gun-control people, we should be seeing an epidemic of violent crime and murder, right? Their argument is that guns are the problem, and if you get the guns out of peoples' hands, we'll all be safer. So if there are more guns, we all must be in more danger, according to them. But they are dead wrong. In fact, violent crime is at a twenty-three-year low. The violent-crime rate has declined every year since 1991. Murder is at a thirty-five-year low, according to the FBI. It looks like something is seriously wrong with the gun-control advocates' arguments.

The cold, hard facts tell us that if citizens are protecting themselves, criminals are going to be less likely to strike because they have something to fear. Let's imagine what would happen if you took every gun away from every law-abiding citizen in the country. That would mean our safety was totally dependent on gun control and law enforcement. Last I checked, the definition of a criminal is somebody who breaks the law. So I'm guessing that if we have gun control, and law-abiding citizens all turn in their firearms, criminals will break that law and hold on to their guns, and then they are going to go out and celebrate, because they know law-abiding citizens don't have guns anymore and can't protect themselves. That would mean they have nothing to fear, or nothing serious anyway, maybe a table knife, a baseball bat, or a teapot. That just shows what flawed logic gun-control advocates have to resort to in order to scare people so they can push their agenda.

I am just glad we have the National Rifle Association (NRA) looking out for us. These antigun groups hate the NRA, but, my friends, the NRA is not the problem in this country. The NRA lobbies for criminals who get caught using a gun to be given the maximum sentence under the law. They lobby for people who are in illegal possession of a gun to be punished according to the law. They say: Put them behind bars. The NRA looks out for the people who buy guns legally by registering them and going through the fingerprinting and the background checks—good, honest people who have committed no crime except wanting to protect themselves according to their constitutional rights.

Why should we fear any law-abiding citizen having a gun? We shouldn't. But antigun groups would make you think that guns are the problem. I can't remember honestly the last time that I heard about a gun getting up by itself and shooting somebody. Can you? But that's what they want to make you believe. They will use anything they can to make their arguments, even if it means making opportunistic use of other peoples' tragedy.

Columbine is the most hateful example of that. Let's be honest. Eric and Dylan, the two people who committed the horrendous murders at Columbine, were not law-abiding citizens. Gun control was not the issue. More laws would never have stopped Eric and Dylan. Does anyone believe for a second that even though they had been planning these depraved murders for six months or more, a few more laws on the books would have made them sit down together and say, "Oh, no, we can't do it, because we will be breaking a few more laws!" No way. There were no amount of metal detectors and no amount of gun laws that could have stopped two people willing to spend months planning a massacre. The real villain lies within the dark psychology of the human being. But politicians try to use restrictive legislation to fix the problem instead of answering the real question. The real question here is how do you prevent something like this from happening?

Darrell Scott, whose daughter Rachel was killed at Columbine, was later asked to testify before the House Judiciary Committee, and he was wise enough to raise the right questions. He asked the members of Congress to look beyond partisan arguments over the NRA and gun control and instead to look within.

"We all contain the seeds of kindness or the seeds of violence," he said. "The death of my wonderful daughter, Rachel Joy Scott, and the deaths of that heroic teacher, and the other eleven children who died must not be in vain. Their blood cries out for answers. . . . I am here today to declare that Columbine was not just a tragedy—it was a spiritual event that should be forcing us to look at where the real blame lies! Much of the blame lies here in this room. Much of the blame lies behind the pointing fingers of the accusers themselves. I wrote a poem just four nights ago that expresses my feelings best. . . .

> Your laws ignore our deepest needs
> Your words are empty air
> You've stripped away our heritage
> You've outlawed simple prayer
> Now gunshots fill our classrooms
> And precious children die
> You seek for answers everywhere
> And ask the question "Why"
> You regulate restrictive laws
> Through legislative creed
> And yet you fail to understand
> That God is what we need!

Those are powerful words. What he was saying to the members of Congress was, "Look, don't cop out and push your personal agenda in the name of my daughter's death." He was telling them it wasn't the gun's fault. I was amazed how quickly fingers began to point at groups like the NRA after Columbine. Darrell Scott put all that to rest when he said, "I am not a member of the NRA. I am not a hunter. I do not even own a gun. I am not here to represent or defend the NRA because I don't believe that they are responsible for my daughter's death."

But the politicians just didn't get it. Bill Clinton couldn't wait to make political hay of Columbine. Al Gore and other liberals around the country were shameless in using the names of the Columbine victims to push their personal gun-control agenda. That just shows how much liberals and politicians like to reduce things down to slogans. They want to take the easy way out and blame guns. But gun control is not the answer. The answer is raising your children with a solid foundation of good, fundamental values so they know the difference between right and wrong.

Think about this for a minute. Let's say that Eric Harris and Dylan Klebold had been raised in households where the rules of the NRA were closely followed. If that had been the case, they would have had the ideals and values of the NRA instilled in them, and they would have learned to respect weapons. They would have been brought up to see that weapons aren't to kill people, they are used to defend yourself or to go hunting. All those kids and that one teacher at Columbine High School probably would have been okay. But instead, Eric and Dylan were brought up on Hollywood pop culture, which is endorsed by the same people who want gun control. I find it amazing that so many liberals could condemn the NRA after Columbine without stopping for one minute to ask if the valueless, immoral swamp that our culture has become is part of the problem. But I guess that would require them to open their eyes and open their minds, instead of sticking with the same tired rhetoric they have been relying on ever since George McGovern ran for president.

Eric and Dylan were the killers, not the guns. But heck, if we are going to go all out to stop violence, we better pull out all the stops. We better stop selling nails, because pipe bombs can be made out of them. We better stop selling propane for people to grill their burgers, because a kid might use it to blow up something. We better get rid of cars, because they can kill people in accidents. We better ban bikes, because people use bikes to get away from crime scenes. We would have to burn all baseball bats, since they can be used as weapons. Oh, and you can forget about motorcycles and crowbars and wrenches.

The small number of people who actually believe that gun control could stop Columbine-type shootings ought to study the example of Australia. The government spent half a billion dollars on a new gun-control program after the Port Arthur massacre, and, in July 1998, gun owners gave up more than 640,000 personal weapons, including semiautomatic

.22 rifles and shotguns. So then what happened? Crime in Australia increased dramatically. Homicide took a slight jump of 3.2 percent over the next twelve months, assaults were up 8.6 percent, and armed robberies jumped an amazing 44 percent, which just proves the point that when criminals have nothing to fear from law-abiding citizens, they will take full advantage. Congratulations, Australia! You have enabled criminals to act out crimes!

That raises a question: What does work? I think we need to work much harder to educate children about guns. That doesn't mean sending some loser around to classrooms, putting up pie charts that give a bunch of stupid statistics. No, I am talking about letting them handle a gun so they can learn what it is and lessen their curiosity. I am talking about an open dialogue with parents and other authority figures who can fill in the blanks and teach them to respect guns. It could be a required mini-course at high school, so that every student learns how to use a gun safely and knows all about how a gun works, so then the curiosity and the mystique are gone.

I think the laws we have now are good. We have background checks, and if you are a criminal, you cannot legally acquire a gun. It's that simple. What else do you want? The answer is to enforce the laws that we already have on the books and stop letting all these criminals get off on probation and plea bargains and parole. If we were enforcing the laws on the books like they should be enforced, and it wasn't working, then I would be for new laws. But people, the point is, why are we wasting our time trying to get more gun control when we don't even enforce the laws we've got?

Why are liberals so afraid to admit that laws are not always the answer? Everyone wants to use Columbine to score political points, but the bottom line is, the Columbine killers lacked moral development. Eric and Dylan veered off the moral road somehow; whether it was because their consciences or self-discipline were not properly developed in them by their parents or peers, who can say? We hardly hear anything at all about how horrible those two killers were, because we were being told constantly how horrible guns are.

If you want to make this country safer, you need to make sure that all law-abiding citizens have the option of owning a gun to protect themselves. Fear is what we need. We need criminals to be afraid, very afraid, that law-abiding citizens are standing there ready to ask, "Do you feel lucky, punk?" If they fear you might have a gun in your house, they are going to think twice before they break in. If they fear you have a gun behind the counter at your place of business, they're going to think twice before robbing you.

Immediately after the September 11 terrorist attacks, the number of people buying guns for themselves jumped dramatically. One New York store owner reported more than a 50 percent increase. Gun sales in the state of Nevada were 61 percent higher the week after September 11 than the week before. More states than ever now have "right to carry" laws, including my home state of Tennessee, one of more than thirty states that now offer that protection to their citizens. There are more guns out there and less crime.

Politicians need to find more money to build prisons so we can lock real criminals up and keep them locked up for a good, long time. But please, stop using kids. People like Sarah Brady, the wife of Jim Brady, who worked so hard on behalf of the Brady Bill, ought to have to answer a question. Go up to Mrs. Brady, or to Bill Clinton, who helped push through the Brady Bill, and ask them if the name Cassie Bernall means anything to them. Ask them if the name Steven Curnow means anything to them. Ask if the name Corey DePooter means anything to them. Or if the name Kelly Fleming means anything to them. Or if the name Matthew Kechter means anything to them. Or Daniel Mauser, or Daniel Rohrbough, or William Sanders, or Rachel Scott, or Isaiah Shoels, or John Tomlim, or Lauren Townsend, or Kyle Velasquez?

I guarantee you, they won't know any of those names. But do you know who those people are? Those are the people who died in the

Columbine shootings. The people who put through the Brady Bill, the people who yell and scream for more gun control, they don't care about these victims. To them the names above are just the names of useful political pawns. They use kids dying to promote their personal agenda. And that's what's sick. When you use kids dying to promote your personal beliefs instead of looking at what the real problem is, that to me is the real crime. Did these victims at Columbine die for no reason? I wonder! Have we really learned anything from the Columbine shootings? Honestly, no. We've made our schools more like prisons, with more security and more metal detectors, and meanwhile, our prisons are getting more like four-star hotels all the time.

CHAPTER 8

What's Wrong with God?

You might not have noticed it, but God has become quite a home-run hitter. He throws a mean fastball, too, and on his good days at least, he can paint the outside corner with a nifty sweeping breaking ball that locks hitters up at the knees every time. What's that? You're not a baseball fan; you prefer football? Well, God kicks field goals from midfield, heaves touchdown passes, and, of course, steps in front of surprised receivers to make interceptions and run them back the length of the field. God also has a booming tennis serve and the sweetest little half volley you've ever seen.

Everywhere you turn in the world of sports, athletes are thanking God and claiming that he was the force behind a homer or a touchdown or a good pitch or a big tackle. Mariano Rivera, the tall, thin Panamanian who has been the best closer in baseball in recent years, put his spirituality on memorable display just after pitching three innings in the New York Yankees' epic Game 7 win over the Boston Red Sox in the 2003

American League Championship Series. An extra-inning homer by someone named Aaron Boone may have won the game for the Yanks, but Rivera did not want to hear any talk about the so-called Curse of the Bambino, which holds that the Red Sox have been cursed ever since Boston owner Harry Frazee sold Babe Ruth to the Yankees after the 1919 season.

"It was the Lord," Rivera told reporters. "The Curse? I don't know about that stuff. . . . I don't believe in ghosts. I believe in the Lord. I had a big conversation with the Man and he came through. That's why I was happy and I was thankful."

God is "not a Red Sox fan," Rivera added. "The Man" told him, the pitcher said, that "we're going to win this game."

Then again, if you asked the Red Sox, they were sure God was on their side. Boston only advanced to the ALCS after rallying from behind to beat the Oakland A's in the Division Series, thanks in large part to Trot Nixon's home run to win Game 3 of that series at Fenway Park. "I got a little gust of wind from the Lord up there and it ended up going out of the ballpark," Nixon explained matter-of-factly afterward.

It used to be that Christian athletes would hold prayer meetings together behind closed doors and mention God only reluctantly. Not anymore. Players like James Thrash of the Philadelphia Eagles football team do not wait to thank God until they have done something remarkable. No, Thrash points skyward by way of thanks after even routine plays. Barry Bonds, the San Francisco Giants' great home-run hitter, points skyward after every homer, which raises the question: Did he thank God after he testified about alleged steroid use before a San Francisco grand jury late last year?

Prayer has become almost as important in sports as the zebras who call the games. Just watch a close college football game and you will see athletes on the sidelines on one knee asking God for help in pulling the game out. Oh, and I love watching boxing when a fighter will step up before the TV cameras after beating the crap out of an opponent and thank

God for allowing him to beat the crap out of the hapless, hamburger-faced loser slumped over in the far corner.

God is one heck of a musician, too, based on what we keep hearing at music awards ceremonies. From Jennifer Lopez to Kid Rock to Eminem, thanking God when receiving an award has become the thing to do. It has gotten so out of hand that at one recent awards ceremony, host Jimmy Kimmel actually used a part of his opening monologue to forbid artists from thanking God in their acceptance speeches.

"God doesn't watch television, and if he does, he wouldn't be watching this," Kimmel said.

What's so interesting to me is the range of people who have jumped on the "Thank you, God" bandwagon. We are not just talking about gospel singers here. Oh no. We are talking about artists who sing about killing people and doing drugs and who have cruel insults for anyone they don't like. I just don't see how you can thank God when you glorify orgies and pimping and hating homosexuals, the way Eminem often does.

Look at Britney Spears. She has become a sex symbol for practically every girl of her generation, and she has thanked God for her success at every step along the way. She started off by acting out every man's fantasy about the girl dressed up in a school uniform, and she kept right on pushing the boundaries in every way possible, always trying to prove, as she said, "I'm Not That Innocent," but always thanking God. She took it a step further when she stripped from an already provocative outfit down to not much more than a thong and a bra during one of her MTV appearances. Don't worry. She didn't forget to thank God after that performance, either.

Britney went on to make another steamy, over-the-top video about wanting to be a "slave for you." It was one of the most popular videos of the year, and I am sure she thanked God after it became such a success. Everyone knows about the 2003 MTV music awards when Britney hit a shock-the-world home run when she and Madonna exchanged an open-mouthed kiss onstage after singing "Like a Virgin." Britney might not have thanked God after that one, but I am sure she would have if she had had a little more time.

The idea of thanking God is now thrown around so lightly, it has almost become politically incorrect not to thank God. Seriously. God has become the "thank-you man" of my generation. Even prayer has become a huge part of pop culture. When you turn on a behind-the-scenes story of almost any musical group or solo artist, they always show the group or artist praying before a performance. Whether you are watching *Oprah* or *E! True Hollywood Story,* the victims or famous people whose lives went bust always seem to end up talking about how they "prayed for God to help them."

Prayer has become so open in sports and entertainment that the national media will cover it without blinking an eye, but what I want to know is: Why is God welcome at every pop-culture event and every sports event, but God is not welcome when it comes to our everyday lives? The more entertainers and athletes want to thank God in passing, the less people want to have to do with God in the spiritual sense. In a typical example, one public high school changed their Christmas Musical to Winter Musical and changed the lyrics of some of the songs from "Christmas" to "winter."

Why is it that God is being taken out of our daily lives in every way? Why is it that God is no longer welcome at graduation ceremonies? Why is it that America is so ashamed of God? Why is it that the few who hate him get their way, but the masses who like him don't stand up and defend him?

The answer to all these questions is painfully simple: America wants freedom from morality. That is why people are so happy to thank God when it is convenient and makes them look cool but so unhappy to take God seriously as a presence in their lives and the lives of people around them. If you talk to the average American and ask if he or she is a Christian, that person will say yes. But if you start to talk to him or her about God, that person will become very uncomfortable. That is because talking about God in a meaningful way can't help but reveal just how far off course we are from what God wants this country to be. People in this country are falling away from God, and they don't want to be reminded that what they are doing is wrong. They just want to live their lives without caring about the moral consequences to their actions.

To that I say: You can run, but you can't hide. We are who we are. There is no freedom from God's laws, only ignorant and arrogant attempts to hide from morality. If you are doing something wrong in your life, many don't want to talk about God. Many want to run from the idea of God and even the idea of right and wrong. That is why real conversations about God are so often avoided in America. If these athletes and pop stars said something meaningful about God, everyone would feel uncomfortable, and that just would not be politically correct.

God is offensive to many people because they know their lifestyle is wrong. But the worst possible thing we could do would be to allow the few who hate God to take God out of our country. The issue of separation of church and state was never about taking God out of America. If it was, then why would God have such a central role in every area of our history? The last I checked, God is in the Pledge of Allegiance, God is on our money, and the president swears on the Bible when he takes the oath of office and so does anyone who testifies in our courts. But for some reason some people don't think God belongs in our lives. I don't get the logic.

God is a huge part of this country and what we were founded on. The point of separation between church and state was about not allowing the government to enforce one faith on the whole country, the way the Church of England did. The leaders of this country wanted to make sure that every single citizen had the freedom to believe in anything he or she wanted. We still have that today. We still have that right. If you don't like God, then don't pray. But that doesn't mean you can't be respectful and allow others to pray for the safety of their child and other children. Does that really hurt you? I don't think so. I am sure we would have far fewer hate crimes in this country if we let the morals that God teaches be given a wider hearing. Why do so many people get so nervous when they hear any mention of the Ten Commandments? I have never heard of a single person's life that was ruined by the Ten Commandments.

If we get rid of God, we will soon be so immoral as a nation that we will never be able to recover from our mistakes. That is, unless we ask God for help. The immoral lifestyle that is present from the ghetto to Wall Street is getting worse day by day. We no longer are choosing leaders who understand that they are not God. Now we have men who are judged by their alma mater instead of their character. Call me crazy, but I don't see why we should trust a man because of where he went to school. I was raised to trust a man by his actions, his convictions, and his faith.

Sure, I know that there are some characters from the Religious Right who make people think Christians are all crazy fundamentalists, and, to be honest, some of those people even scare me. But they are not the norm. What scares me a lot more is the fact that we as a nation are allowing bitter, hateful people to get rid of God. I appeal to my fellow Christians to fight for their beliefs.

The bottom line is, God has not hurt this country, he has only guided us and helped us. If you have a problem with prayer or the Ten Commandments, then check your own life and see if there is something in it that makes you nervous about being reminded of his word. Finally, ask yourself if God has ever hurt you. Ask yourself if the Ten Commandments have ever hurt you. Ask yourself if someone else praying has ever hurt you. The answer I am proud to say is No!

CHAPTER 9

If They All Had Their Way

Everybody has an opinion on affirmative action. But the real question is what does affirmative action mean in 2004? Does it mean fairness? Does it mean quotas? Does it mean playing the victim? The great abolitionist Frederick Douglass was clear that demanding equal rights should never amount to demanding favoritism. He told concerned northerners after the Civil War that they should leave his people alone. "Please mind your own business, and leave us to mind ours," he said. "If we cannot stand up, then let us fall down. We ask nothing but simple justice, and an equal chance to live. . . . Do nothing with us, or by us, as a particular class. We now simply ask to be allowed to do for ourselves."

But that just won't do. Leaders like Jesse Jackson and Al Sharpton have demonstrated that Frederick Douglass was hopelessly misguided and short-sighted. The man was clearly out to lunch. Leaving men to stand or fall on their own is no kind of philosophy! Oh no. Much better to tinker and fiddle and rearrange. The trouble with affirmative action isn't that it has asked too much, we now know, but that it has not asked nearly enough. It's time to drop this foolish caution. We must plunge boldly into this project and have the vision and courage to see it through to its proper and natural conclusion.

Let's start at the top. Well, okay, almost at the top. Obviously we have a big problem with the job of vice president. This won't do at all. Say good-bye to Dick Cheney, Al Gore, Dan Quayle, and heck, even the first George Bush. Say so long to Fritz Mondale, Nelson Rockefeller, Gerald Ford, and Spiro Agnew. Why, you ask? Because they are from the wrong race. I don't care if they are qualified or have proven themselves as leaders. Obviously we can't possibly have vice presidents from the same race as the president, so all of these have to go. Toss out Hubert Humphrey, Lyndon Johnson, and Richard Nixon, while you're at it.

Congress comes next. Sad to say, but we'll have to fire at least half of this crew. Why? Because it looks bad on TV to have so many blue-blood white men in office. How on earth could little Timmy sitting at home watching C-SPAN think he could make anything of himself when all he sees on the floor of the House and Senate are a bunch of white people dressed up in suits? This little boy's life must be over. He could never make anything of himself because he does not see the exact distribution of race in Washington that he sees on his block or in his school or in his family.

So let's ship out anyone with a last name starting with–wait, heads or tails, call it in the air–N to Z. Congressman Bob Ney of Ohio? Way too white. Back to Bellaire for you and your old job as health and education manager for the Office of Appalachia. Anne M. Northup of Kentucky? You're a woman? Okay, you can stay. Eleanor Holmes Norton? Wow, a woman and black? Can we clone you? Charles W. Norwood of Georgia, Devin Nunes of California, Jim Nussle of Iowa, and James Oberstar of Minnesota? Sorry, dudes. Y'all couldn't be any whiter. Be gone. And don't block the door because we have a long line behind you, all the way down to C. W. Bill Young of Florida (nice try with the name, though) and

Don Young of Alaska (the white beard was a good idea). We'll go A to M on the Senate side, so out with all of you. Hold on, Daniel Kahikina Akaka, you can stay, and heck of a nice lei, by the way. Lamar Alexander, Wayne Allard, and George Allen? Later, dudes.

We'll send a bus out to Disneyland and park it right next to the line waiting for the Matterhorn ride. Come one, come all, we'll find a place for you in the Washington power structure. If you're the right color, we'll give you your own letterhead, your own flock of interns, and your own lobbyists (you'll find the white envelope in your top right desk drawer— right, the thick one). What's that you say? You have no interest in government? You think politicians are a pack of scheming liars? No problem. We have a social experiment to conduct here, so no time for limp objections. Step right up, all the way to the back there. Don't forget to pick up your free box lunch.

We're off to a promising start here, but I'm afraid the problem may go even deeper than we had thought. Yes, yes—there's no denying the obvious. We have a major scandal when it comes to clothing. All these suits! As we know, a lot of Americans don't even own a suit. And yet here these senators and congressmen are, showing up on TV in the slickest, most perfectly tailored suits in sight! Forget it. That will not stand any longer. We have to get organized from here on out. A few representatives here and there will be allowed to keep wearing their suits, just for kicks, but most of their colleagues will be assigned new, more tasteful garments. Some will wear fast-food uniforms (name tag included, naturally!). Some will wear factory-outlet sweat suits. Many will be given T-shirts and sweatshirts. Everyone will have to wear electric blue or turquoise or fuchsia sponge-soled running shoes, as garish as possible. Oh, and those dumb-looking fisherman hats that a few misguided Manhattanites think are cool? Two or three of our new congressmen will have to wear those.

Rub your hands together, crack your knuckles, and clap a couple of times loudly, because we're just getting started here. We've inspired little

Timmy watching C-SPAN at home to see what his congressional leaders look like. All is as it should be now. Appearances are everything. The point isn't to fuss and bother over little details like the substance of the laws being drafted and passed. Oh no. The brilliance of the men and women leading our country? All that has to take a backseat to how things look on television and whether little Timmy and every kid of the future will now feel free to achieve greatness because they can see their background equally represented. Little Timmy is now free to become an icon in his own right. Just give him time. There's no stopping him.

Now I know it might seem a little extreme to remake the world so drastically, but this is no time for a failure of nerve. We have to remember, as we are so often told, that it's only possible for people of one race or ethnicity to relate to other people of that race or ethnicity. Seeing things from the other side of the table is not possible. A black man can't possibly have anything in common with a Latino. A woman can't relate to a man. And a working woman certainly can't have anything to say to a housewife.

That goes for age groups, too. How do you think little Timmy feels when he looks at the TV and sees only a bunch of old people in Congress? Timmy is being discriminated against! His age group is wickedly and callously underrepresented! Those old fogeys in the Senate and the Congress and the rest of government can't possibly have the slightest clue what's going on in little Timmy's Britney Spears teeny-bopper world. How on earth can this kid ever be expected to succeed in life? Do we want to rob him of any chance at all to make something of himself? Not on your life. No, we're going to have to get to work and shuffle the deck where age is concerned. This is no time to be sentimental or squeamish.

Chief Justice William Rehnquist? Sorry, we know you've had a long and distinguished career on the bench, but heck, you're going to be celebrating your eightieth birthday in a few months. We're going to have to replace you with Maggie, the baby on *The Simpsons*. Okay, true, she doesn't say much, although you have to agree that the way she sucks on her pacifier is very expressive. But the point is: She satisfies the needs of diversity. Rip a Gap Kids ad out of the Sunday magazine of your local paper, and you'll see the entire new membership for the House Ways and Means Committee. See the little tyke on the right, wearing a blue sweat-shirt? The one with the cowlick and freckles? He'll be the chairman. See the little girl in a daisy-patterned dress? She'll be the deputy.

Little Timmy will be happy with that, although he doesn't like the name of the House Ways and Means Committee. He figures they must really be mean people. Now he's crying. What's that, Timmy? What are you upset about now? Oh, it seems he's been channel-surfing. He got bored watching the Gap Kids kids on C-SPAN and turned over to MTV. He's been staring at the screen for hours now, days actually, and he can't help noticing that everything is seriously out of whack. He's noticing the same trouble with the movies he loves to go and watch, too. But wait. This is a problem that can be fixed!

A lot of those pasty white faces are just going to have to go. There are way too many white people in pop music and especially in the movies. Don't worry. I am an equal opportunity finger-pointer. Yes, there is a se-rious problem with hip-hop. Have you noticed that, like, just about every rap star out there is black? We need equal representation. A few of those displaced congressmen, men with names like Jeffrey and Steven and Daniel, they'll have to pick up a mike and earn an honest living rhyming ^&%$*(&^r with #@%#&) and then coming back with a few %$#%(()&()*&s for good measure. But Jeffrey and Steven and Daniel won't be enough, no, not nearly. We'll need a transgendered Eskimo paraplegic rapper, and a ninety-year-old Arapaho dwarf rapper, and, what the heck, maybe a pair of Honduran conjoined-twin rappers. Boy bands will need a serious makeover, too. What's this stuff about segre-gating by sexes? Enough of that. And enough of this survival of the best-looking. How about some dog-ugly lip-synching pop groups, thrown together as randomly as a jury? Sure they can't sing, and they ain't much to look at, either! Perfect.

Little Timmy will rest so much better at night. He can turn on the radio and gone forever will be oldies' stations and hip-hop stations and classic-rock stations and classical stations. Now you can get a sociology lesson just by flicking on the radio. All ages past and present will be heard. All races will be heard. All types of music will be flowing freely to your ears. Can't you hear how beautiful that sounds? Oh, you say you don't like rap music. Sorry, pal. Like has nothing to do with it. You can't stand in the way of the great blender approach to culture! Barry Manilow and Kenny G and Britney Spears and Mozart and Elvis and Barry White and Coltrane and R.E.M. and U2 are all equals. You have to have an open mind. This is progress!

I know what you're thinking. What if Little Timmy is a sports fan? It just wouldn't do to have him deeply scarred by flipping channels past MTV and catch a football or basketball game by chance. His life would be ruined. He'd wonder if someone had messed with the contrast switch on his TV. He'd find that white people are a small minority in both sports. Two-thirds of players in the NFL are black, and in the NBA the percentage is even higher. And has anyone noticed that there seems to be some kind of bias against short, fat people in professional basketball? Do they think short, fat people don't have feelings? We need to see a lot more centers and power forwards who look just like Jerry's sidekick on *Seinfeld*. No, not Kramer, the tall one, the other one, George. He can't jump? No problem. Jumping is overrated. He can't even see the ball once he's worked up a sweat and his glasses fog up? No problem. Seeing the ball is probably overrated, too. As for the NFL, we need a lot more linebackers with twig arms and spindly little legs and pocket protectors and Coke-bottle glasses. Sure, they wouldn't make many impressive tackles, but it could be fun watching them run away from anyone who moves in their direction, even the TV cameramen.

College sports need some work, too. How come cheerleaders are just about always blonde and sexy? We need more short, dumpy ones. And what's this perfect-complexion stuff. Forget that. They should look like real people. A crater or two can't hurt. Out there on the gridiron, we need diversity, diversity, diversity. Enough of this coordination and prowess and confidence. We want accident-prone athletes! Clumsy ones! Nervous ones! We want them so awkward, they are afraid to leave the huddle because someone might see them.

Little Timmy might have two left feet and no work ethic whatsoever. He might never have practiced, and he might have no talent, but, for goodness sake, he ought to be able to dream, so we've got to nurture his dreams of playing any sport he wants. His parents don't have to teach the work ethic. If he likes a sport, then he ought to be able to play that sport, no matter whether he has any ability or has paid any dues or even knows what it is to work hard and be dedicated. Little Timmy should be able to follow any dream he has, so the same goes for all walks of life. Everyone should be able to do everything. If little Timmy wants to be a federal judge, forget law school. That's too boring. He ought to just walk up and say he's ready to put on his robe. Eye tests for police officers? They are so unfair. If little Timmy wants to be a cop, so what if he's astigmatic and has a trembling hand? Put him in blue. Let him be part of this perfect new world with a Congress and Senate handpicked for every type of diversity you can imagine, and pop music and with movies and sports all taken care of as well. If that doesn't sound good to you, well, then, obviously there's something wrong with you. Trust me. Al Sharpton and Jesse Jackson told me it's time to throw down barriers and change our world, and I wouldn't want to contradict such fine, noble men as those two, now would I?

My point is affirmative action has served its purpose in America, and it's time to move on. As hard as it might be for some troublemakers to admit, affirmative action in our society today represents going backward, not forward. The way it is now, kids in college classrooms look around to see a minority in the next row or over by the window and wonder if he earned the right to be at that school or if he got a leg up. A white student who didn't get into that school now looks at every minority on that campus as the person who might have taken the spot he deserved and solely because he had the right skin color and got to check that little box. Affirmative action was supposed to fight racism, but now it only breeds racism. It's time to let go of the past and embrace the future of America.

The problem is the leaders who have made a name for themselves by talking up affirmative action. They can't let go. They refuse to open their eyes and acknowledge the progress we have made as a nation. When was the last time you heard Jesse Jackson celebrate anything? He has become famous and wealthy because he points his finger and blames whites for all of black people's misfortunes. Heck, I expect three-year-olds to point fingers but not grown adults. Jackson and his friends spend so much time yelling about the past that they can't see the future, let alone see how far we've come as a nation.

Or maybe I'm being too generous. Maybe Jackson and people like him are well aware of how far we've come. That would scare the living heck out of them. Just think about it. If African Americans begin to understand that affirmative action has served its purpose, and decided we can now put the practice behind us, where would that leave Jesse Jackson and the others like him? They would be out of work. Their fight would be over, and their money would be gone. Their arguments would be picked apart by their peers and called "tired and out of date." People like Jackson and Sharpton seem to make their fortunes off the misfortunes of an entire race. So long as they can keep their race believing the only reason they're not all millionaires is because of the evil white man, their pocketbooks will be just fine.

It's time to thank all the brave leaders who opened doors and move on, or we risk having history repeat itself. But this time it's not our parents' or grandparents' fault. It's going to be totally our fault. I am telling you that if we don't start to let men and women, boys and girls, whites and blacks, make it on their own merit, we will continue to breed hatred.

Students will always hold a grudge against anyone in a minority group who got a spot they felt was rightfully theirs. Minorities who worked diligently to make something of themselves will be angry that people are narrow-minded and think they got where they are because of a quota. This never-ending cycle needs to end. If our leaders don't stand up to the Jacksons and the Sharptons, we will never be able to embrace the future. I challenge these men to put their differences aside and allow this generation to figure it out on its own.

CHAPTER 10

Fat America

Americans have become a joke. I don't mean our values or our international leadership or our way of life, all of which make us the envy of the world. I mean us. I mean ourselves. If we all step up to the mirror and ask ourselves honestly what we see, the painful answer will be: too much, way too much. We have become a nation of porkers. We are a country of fatsos. It is a national embarrassment. Just take a look around at the local shopping mall and count the people who take twenty minutes to walk up a normal flight of stairs. Or count how many people look round enough that if they ever wedged themselves into a coach seat on a normal airline, it would take a work crew of eight to dismantle the seat if they were ever going to get out.

We have been reading and hearing reports in the media on the American plague of obesity for years, but the problem just keeps getting worse. It is unbelievable. Back in 1960, only 13 percent of Americans were obese, according to the Centers for Disease Control and Prevention.

That number had almost doubled by 1990, when fully 23 percent of Americans were classified as obese. But the most recent numbers are truly mind-boggling. In 2000, 31 percent of American adults were obese. If that trend has continued at the same rate, and it's a safe bet it has, then by last year more than one-third of all American adults were obese!

Like most problems in this country, the fat epidemic has been discussed to death. We have all heard about how much more fast food Americans eat than they did even a generation ago. To put it in statistical terms, Americans in 1996 spent 40 percent of their food budget on meals they ate outside of the home, compared to only 25 percent in 1970. We have heard over and over again that larger serving sizes are another culprit, though this trend is even more dramatic than most of us know. One serving of McDonald's French fries was good for 200 calories back in 1960—now a regular serving of McDonald's fries is so much larger, it has 610 calories. But somehow, the more we hear about how disgustingly fat we are getting, the more we eat, the less we exercise, and the more of a health problem the supersizing of America becomes.

Fat kills. Up until now, obesity has been the second-leading cause of preventable death in the United States, second only to smoking. But that will change soon enough, as more people kick the smoking habit and more people bloat their way to clinical obesity. Here is a sobering fact: Obesity claims more than three hundred thousand American lives every year, which is a hundred times more lives than were claimed by the cowardly terrorists who attacked this country on September 11. But when it comes to the war on fat, we are nowhere near summoning the kind of national focus and determination we have been able to achieve in the war on terror under President Bush's strong leadership.

I think we can do better. If September 11 taught us anything, it should have been that we can't take our lives for granted. We have to have courage sometimes and show initiative and take action. Most people who are fat have zero activity in their lives, not even regular walking. It is sad but true. They work, if they have jobs, and they eat. That is their day right there: work and eat. They have nothing else. Which is really scary. It flips me out a little, just thinking about it, because it is so sad and depressing. The bottom line is, these people are taking the easy way out. More and more people in this country become fat because it is easy to become fat. You just eat anything you want, without much thought to the consequences, and sit around and don't do anything else.

To me, the epidemic of fat in this country is really a cry for help. People are fat because they are unhappy. As a whole, I think people are less happy than they used to be. If you have problems, or you are feeling depressed, one way to deal with that is to sit down with a pint of Ben and Jerry's and keep on spooning the stuff down until there is nothing left to spoon down. Maybe it won't make you happy, but that much Cherry Garcia or Chunky Monkey sure will distract you for a while. Any good feeling you get from binge eating will last only a short while. Soon enough, you will be feeling down in the dumps again, and so maybe you will head back to the fridge to see what else you can chow down while you sit in front of the TV.

To put it another way, the fat epidemic is a symptom of a lot of other problems we have in this country. Anyone who has watched any TV at all knows that this country has real issues with sex and sex appeal. That relates in a direct way to overeating, especially where women are concerned. Who can blame these women for feeling bad about themselves and feeling that they are ugly or unattractive when they look around and see every single magazine cover and almost every television show advertising some kind of false ideal? They know they could never look like the women on the magazine covers or on TV, even if they starved themselves. They don't have the right bodies, and they don't have the right faces, either, most of the time. They might be beautiful, really beautiful, but not in just the right way that appeals to the sort of people who decide which pretty face to put on their magazine cover or their television show. So what would any normal person do? Give up, of course. If you give up, then you don't have to live with all that pressure to be something you know you can never be. And giving up is really just a form of depression.

Boredom plays a major role, too. A lot of people overeat because it's their way of filling their time without having to face the world and do anything social. It's a vicious cycle where people feel awkward around other people, so they hide away and eat too much, and then they feel even more awkward around other people, so they are even more likely to hide away and eat too much. It all starts with that feeling of being socially inadequate. We all know the feeling. But different people handle it in different ways. If you fall into the trap of isolating yourself by trying to pretend that eating is your friend, it just won't work for you. You will find out soon enough that you have to get beyond a philosophy of: If it feels good, do it. Or, if it tastes good, eat it. That is how the problem starts: Too many Americans are just plain unhappy.

I know what I am talking about here. Believe it or not, I used to be huge. It got to the point where I stopped weighing myself. I knew I weighed more than 270, and I didn't want to know how much more than that I weighed. I was on the tall side, but less than six feet, so that is really plump. And believe me, I heard about it from other kids. They were really cruel.

They called me "Kenny," like Kenny on *South Park*. That one I kind of liked, actually, compared to some of the others. I remember in 1993 when that movie *Free Willy* came out about a killer whale, the other kids took to calling me "Free Benny." They would all laugh about that one. Or later on they made a big production out of telling me I had chester drawers disease.

"Man you got chester drawers disease," someone told me.

"What's that?"

"Your chest has fallen to your drawers."

Then they would all laugh like crazy. There were a lot of others that were about that clever. None of it was what you would call traumatic. But none of it was much fun, either. I remember pretty much every fat-boy insult I ever heard, and I guess I always will, too.

I was embarrassed when people saw me. I was always trying to cover myself up. I would wear these big jackets and big fleeces to cover up as much of me as possible. I remember going on junior-high-school retreats and things like that and never, ever changing my shirt in front of the other guys because I knew they would all make fun of me. Basketball practice was especially bad. I dreaded basketball practice. I mean, I would actively dread it, looking ahead to it all day and just being consumed by worry. Almost every day, we had games between shirts and skins, and I hated it so much when I was on the skins and had to take off my shirt and play basketball that way.

My problem was partly hereditary. I know that. I was active, playing tennis and other sports and always doing something, but I was still really fat. Another problem was I had asthma, and when that got bad, I couldn't take part in sports for weeks at a time. Also, I have somehow broken bones in my body more than ten times already, and always playing sports. Four different years, I was in a cast when Christmas came around. I broke one bone when I was mountain biking in Colorado, another three or four playing basketball, one in a baseball game, and one time I broke my shoulder playing tennis. Don't even ask how I managed that. The point is, each time that happened, I would be out of action for six weeks or so, and I would put on a lot of weight.

One day when I was sixteen something kind of clicked. All my friends were getting girlfriends—we had arrive at that age—and I felt as if I had no chance in that department. I told myself, "Enough is enough." I decided it was time to get really serious about losing some weight, and I set my mind to making some changes. I didn't go on a major diet or anything. No way. I just started running every day, and once I began to lose a little weight, I kind of enjoyed the challenge of losing more. I worked out more. I ran more. I played more tennis. I wanted to play tennis in college, and I knew I had to make a decision: either I lose the weight, or it was time to quit. I liked tennis too much to quit.

Before too long, I looked like a totally different person and had to go out and buy a whole new set of clothes. Nothing fit, especially not the belts. The best moment came when I got on the scale to weigh myself, and I had dropped below 200 pounds. That was a big day. Everybody was thrilled for me. They were wigging out. They knew how hard I had worked to lose that much weight. We all went out that night and celebrated with a steak dinner at Benihanas.

I remember noticing a major difference in how people perceived me. So many people would make supportive comments. They would constantly be coming up and complimenting me, saying things like, "Hey, man, you're looking great, congratulations." That helps keep your motivation high to lose the weight. You never hear of anybody walking up to someone who has lost a lot of weight and saying something like, "Dude, you're still fat!" I think it's an automatic positive.

Exercise is obviously the best way to lose weight, but people try all sorts of different things. They have tummy tucks or staple their stomach or who knows what else. Or you have people who buy pills on late-night TV because they think some pill can save them from being fat. Weight loss has become a multimillion-dollar industry, but few of the products work. The only thing that works is watching what you are eating and making sure you get more exercise. Now, a few people out there are several hundred pounds overweight, but that is a special category. Most people with weight problems are like I was, maybe a hundred pounds overweight, or eighty, and if that is where you find yourself, you can fix the problem yourself.

You can almost equate obesity with the overabundance of channels on television. The more we have to watch, the more we put in our bellies, and the less we do other than sitting there watching TV. Next year, we will all have two hundred channels, and it will just go up from there. The Internet will give us tons more Web sites that can entertain us or at least suck up our time. Plenty of people spend their whole lives just sitting there, staring at one screen or another. Their whole life revolves around watching TV or staring at their computer screen. They hardly ever go outside. They hardly ever walk. They hardly ever do anything active. It's like they sit down one day and never get up. People blame their obesity on food, but I don't think that's it at all most of the time. They are not obsessed with food, they are obsessed with sitting down and never getting up. They are more obsessed with indulging themselves in TV and the Internet.

So what does that mean? Peoples' social lives have dropped down drastically, and they substitute a bond they feel with the Internet or TV. That's why you see a show like *Friends* do so well, many people have this sad, desperate desire to feel some kind of bond with other people, even if it is completely a false bond. People are so passive, they rely on the Internet for everything, even their social life. Everything is brought to them. You can almost never leave your house and get by just fine, and some people call that being normal!

Even a four-year-old can understand that there is some pretty basic math here to consider: If you do nothing and your body is not burning off calories, you are going to gain weight. The less active you are, the less you can eat without plumping up like a butterball. What is so hard to understand about that? Really it should be a simple problem to fix, but what's going to happen is people are going to keep getting bigger and bigger and health-care prices are going to get higher and higher. It's going to turn into a worse and worse problem. It already costs millions a year to treat diabetes and other diseases tied to weight gain. We as a society will have to pay big, and it's all because people refuse to stay active.

Too often, fat people play the part of the victim. They always have someone or something else to blame for being fat. But in my opinion, that's bogus. If you are fat, then eat less and start working out. It's that simple. But people blame being fat on their childhood or their upbringing. They blame their parents or mean kids at school. But I have zero tolerance for that kind of cop-out. I was in the same situation that they're in, and the bottom line is, it is their own fault. They can't blame society or mean people for giving them low self-esteem. If their metabolism is lower than somebody else's, so what? That just means they have to watch it and be more careful. That just means they have to take responsibility for their own lives and find a way to get active.

CHAPTER 11

Who Will Stand Up
for Old People?

We have a real problem in this country with old people. It makes sense that we would not know how to deal with old people, since we live in such a youth-oriented, youth-obsessed culture. We worship speed. Whatever is newer and faster must always be better, so older and slower must therefore be bad. I think that is a big part of why Americans do not show much respect for old people and instead take the attitude that they are bothersome and annoying.

The really sad part is how we convince ourselves that old people can't teach us anything. Again, this has to do with speed. If a dial-up Internet connection already seems hopelessly slow and out-of-date, and we are forever looking to the new thing, it may be inevitable that we tend to write off old people as irrelevant and useless. My generation is the worst. We think we know everything and no one can tell us anything. There is always some young whippersnapper coming up who thinks he can do it better and is smarter than the old CEO who has been with the company for twenty years.

Part of that may relate to workplace politics. People in my grandfathers' generation tended to stick with the same company for thirty or forty years, if they liked their jobs at all. That led to resentment from people in my father's generation, because a lot of times they had a hard time getting promoted because older people were keeping their jobs for so long, so there was never any turnover. That seems out of date now. People change jobs all the time, and who really cares what older people do anyway? But I think there is still some lingering resentment of the men who control companies after sticking around for a long, long time, even if their years of experience could just as easily be seen as a positive.

A lot of the big scandals that hit companies would never have happened if people were less eager to do things their own way. If you pay attention, you will see that the people involved in those corporate scandals tend to be in their forties or fifties, not in their sixties or seventies. You don't see many people past sixty going to jail for white-collar crime. We don't spend time appreciating what older people have done for this country or what they've accomplished, and it's because of this misplaced faith that we have all the answers. We're right all the time. We're new school, and they're old school. We are reality, and they are not. But that just shows how foolish we are. We do not even know what we are losing by ignoring history or the wisdom and guidance of people in a position to offer both. We've lost a lot of that, I think.

Instead, we see older people being pushed out of companies all the time. It's really sad when you can get pushed out of your own company, which carries your last name, because the youngbloods think that they can do it better. They may be able to grow quickly, too, at least for a while. But then they are likely to come down to earth in a hurry. Look at the stock market in recent years. Companies tend toward the extremes, going through the roof or bone dry. If you look at the ones that are steady, middle-of-the-road companies, nine times out of ten they are companies that have been around for years and have good people in top positions with plenty of experience and plenty of continuity.

Wal-Mart has been a great success story, and it has been able to sustain that success. That is partly because the corporate culture at Wal-Mart is to make the most of all of your assets, including the wisdom of people who have been working for the company for years. That all started with Sam Walton, who oversaw the chain's growth from its beginnings with one store in Rogers, Arkansas. He kept his family involved, and they learned from people who were older than them. The younger ones respected the opinions of the older ones and learned lessons from where the older ones had failed. But we as a society do not do that now.

Last year's World Series might have made a few people think, though. Baseball is a young man's game. Oh, especially if you are a left-handed pitcher, you can hang on for a while. Roger Clemens decided to pitch this year for the Houston Astros and celebrate his forty-second birthday in uniform, but he's a future Hall of Famer. Mostly, baseball is a game full of young faces, like those on the Florida Marlins team that shocked the Yankees in the World Series. Hold on, though. The Marlins' secret weapon was no kid. He was their manager, Jack McKeon, and how can you not like that guy? He was considered a total has-been. He wasn't even in baseball early last season. He was sitting at home in Elon, North Carolina, a grandfather nine times over, when the Marlins called in May and asked him to become the oldest man ever to take a managing job. He turned seventy-three last November.

"When he was home, he was helping out the high-school baseball team and pitching girls' fast-pitch softball," McKeon's son, Kelly, told reporters during the World Series. "He manages the team like he wants us to raise our grandchildren. He loves this bunch of guys and their unselfishness."

McKeon may be old, but his young players swear by him. They were raving about him after the Marlins won the Series. They said he taught them about respect. They said they learned about much more from him than just baseball: He taught them about life, they said, and that made their baseball better. It was how to be a person, how to deal with the media, how to be a team, how to be a family on the road. That all added up to a baseball team that had something special and showed it when things counted in October.

We could use a few more stories like that in the corporate arena. Instead you have the Enrons and the Worldcoms. You have fifty-year-old men who are multi-multimillionaires who for some reason never learned that if you aren't happy with $100 million, you sure as heck aren't going to be happy with $150 million. That is already way more money than you could ever spend, and if it is not satisfying you, the problem is with you, not the number of zeroes after the dollar sign. If you are looking for contentment, run the company the right way, and you should be able to find satisfaction. But we don't think that way. We have never learned that. Instead, corporate executives act like toddlers, wanting whatever the next guy has, plus one. When is enough enough? If we ever wise up and learn that contentment and happiness are worth fighting for, they are worth learning about, we just might get around to seeking out old people and benefiting from their experience and perspective.

The politicians are the worst. They do not just ignore old people, they exploit them. Old people vote in large numbers, and there are more and more of them all the time. Back in 1900, only 4.1 percent of the population was sixty-five years or older. As late as 1950, only 8.1 percent were that age. But by 1997, 13 percent of the U.S. population was elderly, and that means we're talking about 34.1 million people. The median age has moved up, too. It was only twenty-three back in 1900. By 1980, it was up to thirty, and by 1996, it was thirty-five. According to the people who get paid to guess at these things, the median age will be all the way up to thirty-nine by 2030.

Politicians are well aware that old people vote in droves. They are the most solid voting bloc, and they can be counted on to come out year after year and election after election. That is partly because if you are retired, you have more time on your hands, so you look forward to small tasks like getting your mail. Going to vote on Election Day can be the highlight of your week. That also means older people are available to volunteer for a candidate and do other charity work.

Politicians know how much they need old people, which is why every election cycle you can count on a fresh scare over Medicare or Social Security or an issue like that. If I had a dollar for every time I heard Medicare was going bankrupt or Social Security was going to run out of funds, I'd be rich. Politicians make both those claims every time an election is coming up because they want to scare the hell out of old people. They know that is the way to get them to vote. But in reality, there's no way Social Security is going to go bankrupt. It couldn't happen. The consequences would be too disastrous. So if it happened on your watch, your political career would be over.

If anything, politicians should be scared of old people, because if they don't keep them happy, old people are going to vote against them. It's amazing how politicians have turned the tables and made sure old people were good and scared. What they're doing is called lying. I am sure if you asked most politicians behind closed doors, "Is there really any chance Social Security will go bankrupt or Medicare checks won't show up?" and they answered honestly, they would all be saying, "Nope. But it gets people to vote, so we'll bring it up." I think that's really evil.

One reason politicians can get away with that kind of stunt is that people in general would prefer to ignore old people. There is a feeling that they are has-beens and nuisances. Young people complain all the time that old people are a bother or that they drive too slow. And you know what? They have a point there. If we were not so eager to ignore old people, and hope they just keep quiet and stay out of sight, we would respect them enough to look at the realities of their lives. That could mean making some policy decisions old people might not like very much.

Politicians really should take some brave stances toward old people, and driving is a perfect example. There are a lot of old people who have no business driving. You have tests for people when they are sixteen and seventeen and first getting their licenses. But after you hit a certain age, you don't even have to take a driving test to get your license renewed. The new one just comes in the mail. That is fine if you are, for example, a normal, healthy forty-year-old man. But if you are over sixty-five, it is basically up to you to decide when you can't drive anymore, and that's crazy!

Look at how many wrecks happen that involve old people whose motor skills are not what they used to be. I have older family members who have no business driving; somebody needs to take away their licenses. But they are stubborn, and they won't listen to their family. In those cases, all too often someone like that is going to kill themselves or get someone else killed. But politicians won't pass a law requiring anyone sixty-five or older to take a motor-skills test every year or two. Politicians would never in a million years want to risk ticking off old people, so they sit back and do nothing and more people die.

The politicians are doing no one any favors with their cowardice, least of all the old people themselves. As we all know, motor skills decline and sometimes they can fade rapidly. All it takes is one stroke, or one mini-stroke, or even a minor heart attack, and your reaction time can slow down several notches. That puts other people at risk and creates a major hazard. But politicians won't touch that one with a ten-foot pole. They will scare the heck out of old people, to make sure they vote, but when it is time to take a stance and save lives, they are no-shows.

The politicians should remember George Weller. He is the eighty-six-year-old man who mistakenly hit the gas in the parking lot of a Santa Monica farmer's market last summer and killed ten people and injured more than sixty others. The California Highway Patrol investigation of the tragedy found that Weller had his "eyes open, hands on the steering wheel at the ten o'clock and two o'clock positions" and that driver error, not mechanical error, was the only conceivable explanation for what happened. Weller issued a statement saying he was heartbroken over the incident, which he called an accident.

There was a huge debate after that, because his motor skills were obviously terrible and he got very confused between the gas and the break. He was sober and didn't have any drugs in his system; he was just old and frail and shouldn't have been driving. You would think after something like that, politicians would pass laws to avoid a repeat of the same terrible incident. But somehow that never happened. They talked about it, but then it just died out.

Some people just don't want to be bothered. If they take away your father's or mother's license, who is going to drive them? You are! So part of it is selfish. I think that is where leadership should come into play. Elected officials are supposed to be leaders and are supposed to look ahead and face problems head-on. So if we are not responsible enough to ask our elderly parents when they are going to stop driving, our elected officials should be the ones to solve the problem. But I don't see too many forty-five-year-olds embracing that one, because they don't want to have to drive Mom and Dad around all the time. So they figure they'll just let it go and keep their fingers crossed and hope no one gets killed. Some people might call that respect, but another name for it is not wanting to get involved. Another name for it is killing me softly.

CHAPTER 12

Anti-Americanism Is Our Problem Too

'Ve never been more proud of my country than I was watching the way we pulled together after September 11. We were in pain. We were in shock. But we united behind President Bush's leadership and showed the world just how strong a country we are. I only wish we had done a better job of following through on that sense of purpose we all felt in the first few months after the World Trade Center came tumbling down. I only wish conservatives in particular had done a better job of staying focused on what was important and what wasn't important.

We embarrassed ourselves with the way we handled some aspects of the buildup to the war in Iraq. We behaved so childishly, we alienated ourselves from people around the world. Take the infamous case of "Freedom fries." Look, I understand. I jumped on that bandwagon, too. We saved France's rear end. Not just in World War II but in World War I, too. Now we need them, and they won't help us? I thought that was despicable. But it doesn't help our national interests to do things like rename the food in Washington to Freedom fries.

Let's be honest. If the war in Iraq was so important, why on earth did congressmen think they had enough time to pass a law declaring that they were going to change the menu in the House cafeteria from French fries to Freedom fries? That's the most childish thing I've ever seen our government do. Think about it from the standpoint of other countries around the world. Or think how we would have reacted if another country had changed the name of an American product or an American food in some way to denounce us for not going along with them. Every single talk-show host in America would have had a field day with that. Every politician would have jumped on that one, saying things like, "What losers! What a pathetic way for them to handle themselves! Renaming a food? How childish is that?" But that's exactly what we did.

We also acted like children in saying, "You're either with us or you're against us, and France isn't with us." I think if you look at it honestly, it's obvious that the French weren't with us, but they weren't necessarily against us. We should have respectfully disagreed. Instead we took it to a second-grade level. Our reaction was pretty much, "Well, fine, screw you, and we're going to show how much we don't like you." If you want to tell people not to buy their wine and cheese, fine. But don't waste the taxpayer's time discussing and voting on a law about Freedom fries. Why should any other country even listen to us after that? Why should they respect what we have to say?

This wasn't some wacko, fringe group doing this. This wasn't a bunch of crazies. These were our *elected officials* passing a law in Washington. These were our elected officials completely forgetting that it's in our self-interest to treat other people the way we expect other people to treat us. That was really the issue. We expected other countries to jump on the America bandwagon. We expected them to bow down to us. But we couldn't even find a way to treat them with basic respect. We couldn't even find a way to hear them out and try to understand their thinking. We basically just told them, "We're the superpower, so you should do what we say."

Other countries don't always think we're right, just like we don't always think other countries are right. Why should we expect anything else? What's important is that if we don't quite see eye to eye on something with our allies, we can leave the discussion on good terms even if they don't jump on board. Did we really think that because we made so much noise about Freedom fries that was going to help us convince the leaders of France to throw up their hands and say, "Oh, well, okay, we'll jump on the America bandwagon now. Sorry we didn't see it your way before." No. They were going to throw up a brick wall. Just like we did.

It's just not realistic for any country in the world to expect every other person in the world to agree with what it does. There will always be some people who respectfully disagree. We're lucky enough as Americans to be able to flex our muscles. We are one of the least vulnerable countries in the world. We felt vulnerable after September 11, but that was all relative. Compared to other countries, we are less vulnerable, and that shapes our sense of the possible. The more vulnerable a country is to terrorism, the less likely it is to take a bold position on the war on terrorism or the war in Iraq.

We even told our own people that it was dangerous to visit Europe. We put out travel advisories telling American citizens to get the heck out of these countries because they might be targets of terrorism. We did that at the same time that we were criticizing these countries for not supporting us. But hold on a minute. If we don't think our own citizens are safe in that country because of the threat of retaliation, why should we be surprised when these countries are reluctant to get involved because they know they might be retaliated against? I am sure that more countries would have jumped on board with us if the people there were as safe as we are in this country. They would have been more willing to flex their muscles. But they aren't as safe, and we know it. That's why I think it was very arrogant and cocky for us to have expected these other countries to jump when we said jump.

The worst part is, that arrogance and cockiness have given people in other countries an excuse. There are always going to be knee-jerk anti-American fanatics around. There will always be a few radicals and permanent-student types around who want to bad-mouth anything and everything about Americans. But I think that in the last year or two, we've seen anti-American sentiment growing because of this widespread sense that you're either with us or you're against us, and if you're not 100 percent with us all the time, we're going to boycott you.

We need to remember how the world reacted to September 11. At the time we were preoccupied with ourselves and understandably so. But people all around the world reacted as if they thought September 11 was an attack on them, too, not just on America. You saw people march in Germany by the hundreds of thousands. You saw people in France hold candlelight vigils. You saw people in Canada crying. The Germans and French and Canadians were totally 100 percent on our side. They willingly sent troops to Afghanistan to fight the Taliban. That was not an easy decision for some of those countries, especially Germany, where sending troops abroad remains very controversial. But they saw the issue clearly, and they saw the need to act clearly. They thought it was important to help us strike directly against Osama bin Laden and his bases in Afghanistan.

We have to keep in mind that September 11 was a black-and-white issue. So was the campaign against bin Laden. Those issues were unusual in how clear-cut they were. They were simple and easy to understand. Any child could grasp the basics. There was a group called the Taliban. There was a leader named Osama bin Laden, whose followers hijacked two planes with innocent people and crashed them into two buildings. There was another plane hijacked the same day, and luckily the passengers helped bring that plane down in Pennsylvania before it could crash into another building. Then there was a fourth hijacked plane that hit the Pentagon. It was all so stark and simple. Four planes were hijacked by terrorists to kill innocent people, and why? It was just because they hate Americans. And that is what I would call true anti-American sentiment.

What happened during the months before the Iraq war was something very different. Americans should not expect other countries to support every war that we fight. We have the option not to support Germany if it goes to war with somebody. Or not to support France if it goes to war with somebody. Or not to support Canada. So why do we expect all these other countries to jump on board with us any time we go to war with somebody? It's not a fair expectation. Sure, to us it looked as if they were being lame. We were probably right about that. But they had their perspective, too.

The big change between before September 11 and afterward was in how we as Americans perceived the world. Before September 11, we had the feeling we were completely safe. We could be pretty sure that neither Canada nor Mexico was going to send troops over the border to attack us. We could defend ourselves from any other attack because we're divided from other countries by two bodies of water. We were not going to have a major war on U.S. soil unless it was nuclear. So we could flex our muscles a lot more than other countries around the world. That made us feel invincible. Until September 11, I think we even felt exempt from terrorism. Now we have been shown that that was never true. No major country can be exempt from terrorism. But wait. There's hasn't been one attack since September 11. No more planes have been hijacked. No more buildings have been knocked down. We are not as afraid of that happening now as we were two years ago.

However, countries like Germany and France are actually much more vulnerable to terrorism than we are. Even more so for Saudi Arabia and Israel. They are also much more vulnerable to other countries attacking them because they are so close together. The only thing dividing them from their neighbors is literally a line in the sand. It's just not fair for us as Americans to expect them to jump on board every time we say jump? It's not fair. It's not right. And it's not smart.

President Bush had to take a strong stance. He was right to say that you're either with us or against us when it comes to fighting terrorism. That rhetoric was important to show the world—and terrorists—how committed we are to winning this struggle. But the main thing is to be smart. We don't have to believe all our own rhetoric. We hurt only ourselves by falling into this mentality that we'll go it alone and screw you if you don't want to join us. We hurt only ourselves by failing to take into consideration how much tougher it is for leaders in these other countries to convince their people to go to war. We hurt only ourselves by forgetting that these other countries are much more likely than we are to face direct retaliation for joining us in war.

But this argument goes beyond mere tactics. It really gets down to the nature of debate. Sometimes disagreement is a good thing. Sometimes the best advice comes from someone challenging you to question your own thinking. American leaders need to understand that people are not your enemy just because they disagree with you on something. Heck, I've disagreed with my family and friends a million times. I've disagreed with people within my own party. That doesn't mean they're my enemy. And just because a country doesn't agree with us doesn't mean they are our enemy.

Until we change that mind-set, anti-American sentiment is going to grow. Sometimes people don't see eye to eye. But we were not willing to accept respectful disagreement from countries that did not support our approach to going after Saddam Hussein and his evil regime. I think that's going to come back to haunt us. Let's be frank: We won the Iraq war basically by ourselves. We didn't really need any help militarily. But what happens next time? We might really need countries like France and Germany and Canada to fight a bigger war. What happens when we actually need them for air support to refuel our planes over their territory?

We burned some bridges. Places like Germany and France and even Russia may hold that against us next time.

Elected officials pick what they want to do. That's their job. They pick the wars they want to fight. They pick the people they want to consider their enemies. If our elected officials can pick all of that, why can't the elected officials in other countries pick the same things? Don't our ideals of freedom of ideas and freedom of expression apply to them as well? We preach these ideals here at home, but that rings pretty hollow when we denounce these other countries for not going along with us, basically telling them, "Hey, don't think that when we preach about what's so great about our country, we mean for that to apply to you, too."

The fact was, Iraq wasn't a black-and-white issue. There was a lot of complex history there. There were a lot of reasonable questions that could be raised there. Heck, some people could have said that we were terrorists because we helped Saddam Hussein get weapons back in the 1980s when we were backing him in his war against Iran. He was our ally when he was gassing the Kurds. We knew he was torturing his own people, killing people based on his personal whims, but we supported him then because we thought Iran presented more of a danger to us than Saddam did. We've made a lot of other difficult decisions to support tyrants and dictators when we thought it was in our best interests to do so.

That's how it is. Sometimes a president has to hold his nose and make difficult choices. But we can't expect other countries to ignore our track record. We can't expect other countries to forget that our record on following through in other countries isn't exactly great. We armed the Mujahideen in their struggle against the Red Army in Afghanistan and then left them on their own. We told the Kurds to rise up against Saddam after the first President Bush's war in Iraq and then left them on their own. Time and again, we've left people to deal with the consequences of our actions and inactions. We walk away, and the people we tried to suppress come back to kill the people who sided with us, and we say, "Oops, sorry." Or look at something like the Iran-Contra deal. We have a long record of jumping in and jumping out. We have a habit of changing our rationale from one time to another and expecting our allies to keep accepting that.

Other countries might have seen weapons of mass destruction as a foggy issue. If I'm the leader of another country, am I going to jump behind America on that? Maybe not. Maybe that leader is looking out for his own citizens' protection. Is that a good idea? Probably is! Because we look out for our people first as well. That's a leader's job. France, Germany, and Russia looked at Saddam Hussein as a horrible person and a tyrant, but I don't think they'd come along in their perceptions of him as far as we had after September 11. If we're honest with ourselves, we'll admit that before September 11, we didn't like Saddam Hussein, we thought he was a tyrant and a horrible leader—but we didn't go after him. We pushed to do that only after September 11.

What exactly changed? To us, it was clear. Everything looked different after September 11. The danger that Saddam might do something seemed different. The need to strike out against him became much more profound. Our eyes were opened to the possibility of what Saddam could do because we saw what other terrorists did with those two planes. But these other countries around the world that didn't jump on the bandwagon to attack Saddam probably looked at Iraq much as we did before September 11. They saw Saddam as a dictator and a tyrant but not as someone presenting an imminent threat to the world.

All they were doing was seeing Saddam the way we did on September 10. But our minds had changed by September 11, September 12, and every day afterward. We decided we were going to get terrorism before it showed its face to us again. We were basically making an educated guess. So it was not fair for us to expect other countries to go along with that. It's just like we can't really understand what the Israelis and the Palestinians think of suicide bombings and these unending terrorist attacks against each other. We can't know because we've never experienced that.

No one likes to be bossed around. No one likes to be told what to do, America included. We don't like it when other countries tell us what to do, do we? Absolutely not! We get really angry and irritated. So why shouldn't we expect other countries to react the same way? Especially with countries that have been our friends for decades, like France and Germany. This is a time when we should be trying to build relationships all over the world, given the huge challenge of fighting the war against terrorism. Instead, our with-us-or-against-us attitude was a good way to destroy relationships with other countries.

I actually find it very strange how quick we have been to write off some countries. This goes back to the whole Freedom fries episode. France doesn't agree with us, so we write them off. Germany disagrees with us, so we denounce them. Canada disagrees with us, so we call them pathetic. If you write off counties that quickly, what do you expect? Of course they're not going to like you.

We've seen so much anti-American sentiment around the world because we've become so arrogant and cocky and so aggressive, which is fine, but we still have to have diplomatic ties to these other countries. We still have to have some kind of understanding. We still have to reach out and show we're trying to understand their nervousness and their worries about their own citizens. We haven't done a good job of that, which is just plain bad policy. American leaders need to change our policy, to make it more accepting of people who disagree with America. We need to make sure that we are willing to overlook some of our differences with other countries. Most of all, we need to understand that people in other countries may not look at the war on terrorism the same way that we do.

They were with us after September 11. They understood the urgency of our need to take action against Osama bin Laden. They felt compassion for us. That was an issue that was easy for everyone to understand, easy for everyone to see the same way. The Iraq war was something else completely. But I think when other situations develop, we will find that these other countries will support us if we can make a case that's simple and shows the threat to other countries as well.

It all comes back to communication being a two-way street. If we look at these issues through the eyes of other countries, it will be easier for us to understand how they see our concerns and problems. We need to look at the predicaments these other countries have. We need to look at the economic and political realities that explain the actions of foreign leaders. Sure, some countries were playing politics, or trying to screw us, but their leaders have to look out for their own people, too, just like America puts Americans first. Sometimes that puts leaders in other countries in a difficult situation. We need to give them room to maneuver, not make their lives more difficult.

If we keep up with this rhetoric and doing stupid things like supporting the change to Freedom fries and boycotting products from Germany and France and Canada and making fun of them or lashing out at them for not supporting us, then one day when we really need them, they are not going to be there. And you know what they are going to say? They'll be saying, "Screw y'all. You're so arrogant. You're so cocky. You're getting what you deserve. You deserve this torture you're getting. You deserve this torment you're getting." And there will not be too many countries that feel sorry for us because we are so demanding and so inflexible in our decisions.

So any time people talk about anti-American sentiment around the world, keep in mind that we've brought a lot of it on ourselves. We're expecting the world of other people to do what we say without looking at it from their perspective. And that is what is alienating America from getting along with other countries. We've got to stop it soon. Otherwise, my generation is going to pay the price. It will fall on my generation to live with the consequences. These older leaders are being so arrogant and so obnoxious in the way they are treating other countries, but my generation will be left to pick up the pieces.

PART III

A Political Virgin

CHAPTER 13

Why I'm a Virgin

Some people laugh when I tell them I'm twenty-two and have never had sex. Other people don't believe me. I have actually had conversations that took hours to convince a person that I was not joking when I said I was a virgin. But you know what? I'm proud I'm a virgin. I'm glad I'm a virgin. I don't even mind talking about it. So maybe you wonder: Why am I a virgin? It's actually very simple. I am a virgin because I choose to wait until I get married. I have seen so many before me wish they could go back and choose abstinence. A lot of young people don't feel they have a choice. They think there's something wrong with being a virgin. Honestly, that is totally untrue. Choosing to remain a virgin until you are married does not make you part of some cult. It is a choice that many others and I have decided is right for our lives.

Sure, there's a lot of peer pressure. From TV to magazines to movies, the world preaches that it's not normal to be a virgin, especially by the time you've reached your junior or senior year of high school. I'm writing this to tell you it doesn't have to be like that. Being a virgin doesn't make me better than someone else who is not a virgin, but it doesn't make them better than me, either. I'm as red-blooded as the next guy. Maybe more so. But I'm not going to let somebody else's half-baked ideas about what's cool or what's the norm keep me from being true to my idea of what's right for me. The problem is, kids are told that it's a rite of passage to get laid as soon as you reach puberty, but that assumption is not even remotely true. It does not have to be that way.

Part of my decision has to do with my parents. They taught me from an early age that virginity is an option. They didn't try to freak me out about sex or scare me. They didn't harp on the dangers of having sex, warning me constantly that I could get a girl pregnant or get some horrible disease and ruin my life. They put sexuality into a larger context. They taught me to think of virginity as a way of life. "You are worth waiting for, and you should try to find somebody who's worth waiting for," they told me.

It's tough, because everything is about sex. You channel-surf or go to the magazine stand, and it's just sex, sex, sex. The reality is: Sex sells. It gets people to pick up a magazine or watch a stupid television program that has nothing going for it but enhanced breasts and loud music. There's nothing we can do about that. All I'm saying is, if there are piles and piles of glossy magazines with articles on "10 Ways to a Better Orgasm" and "How to Please Your Man," then somebody should write an article entitled "How to Be a Sexy Virgin" or "10 Steps to Abstaining from Sex" or "Safe Sex Means Saving Yourself for Marriage."

That example needs to be out there, too. It used to be. Just ten or fifteen years ago if you were having sex before marriage, you were considered by many to be a slut or a male whore. Now it's the other way around. If you're not having sex, people think you're not normal. They think there must be something wrong with you. We need to get back to saying, "Look, there is no safe sex except abstinence." But now we are giving young people a false sense of hope and security. Nothing is foolproof. Not condoms. Not birth control pills. They don't work all the time.

It's a lie to say "safe sex" when talking about having sex. The government is lying to us, the sex-ed teachers are lying to us, the condom companies are lying to us, and we're using the lie to make everybody feel "safer." As long as sexual magazines are rolling of the presses, as long as condom companies are selling condoms because their ads in magazines and on TV are working, these people are going to keep preaching that there is such a thing as "safe sex." That is their job, and we should not expect anything less from them. These people are going to promote sex in any shameless way they can to make one more buck.

Just look at how much we've changed in recent years. Remember when the Murphy Brown TV character was having a kid out of wedlock, and Vice President Dan Quayle gave a speech in San Francisco raising questions about that? The sound bite was repeated over and over, as if he had made some huge faux pas, but all he said was, "It doesn't help matters when prime-time TV has Murphy Brown, a character who supposedly epitomizes today's intelligent, highly paid professional woman, mocking the importance of fathers by bearing a child alone and calling it just another lifestyle choice." The controversy after Quayle said that was huge, and ugly, and it might even have cost him a shot at the presidency. But you know what? He was right to tell the country that fathers are important.

That was only twelve years ago. Now look at what we have: *The Bachelor* and *Average Joe.* We have all these dating shows where it's raining hookups. We have *Friends,* where it's no big deal to live together if you're not married, and it's okay to have sex if you're not married. Everybody has pretty much slept with everybody on that show, right? It's okay for the Rachel character to have a kid out of wedlock. They make it look like it's easy. Well, it's a thirty-minute sitcom. Of course it's going to be easy! Remember, Hollywood writes the script. We can't always write the script to our own lives. But people get sucked into this idea that it's no big deal if you have a kid out of wedlock. It's no big deal if you have sex before marriage.

Look at all the sitcoms, and you get the definite feeling everybody is doing it. But life is not a sitcom. You can't solve your problems in thirty minutes. There are consequences to your actions. There are consequences if you're seventeen years old and you get pregnant. You either have to live with the trauma of having had an abortion; or you have to drop out of school, have the kid, find a way to fend for that kid, and also deal with the father and whether he is going to be a father figure or not. There are consequences to having sex, and sometimes that includes suffering. Even if you don't get pregnant, there is the possibility of AIDS and other sexually transmitted diseases. Nobody wants to hear about the negatives. Nobody wants to talk about it, because that's not the cool thing to do. What's supposedly cool is talking about being experimental, having a threesome, engaging in group sex, or having multiple sexual partners.

People take something important like sex and fall into this crazy mentality of, "Well, you wouldn't buy a car before you test-drive it." Like, you wouldn't want to get married to someone if you hadn't gone to bed with her first, because what if she was not a good ride? Well, sex is not buying a car. But it's being brought to a level where people get the message that it is no big deal to have casual sex. Now it's like going to the soft-drink machine and picking out a flavor; if you don't like one, then just try another. Somebody needs to play devil's advocate. Somebody needs to say that condom companies tell you it's safe sex because they want to sell condoms and make money, not because it's true. Somebody needs to say that sitcoms have nothing to do with reality. That's not life. Life is when you have a kid, and it's a day-in and day-out responsibility, twenty-four hours a day and seven days a week.

Sex education has to change, too. We spend taxpayer's money to teach schoolchildren about so-called "safe sex." Kids are given tips on getting birth control and using condoms correctly. We give out free condoms. Here's why I think that is missing the boat: If you have eighth-graders, guys and girls together in a co-ed situation, and you teach them how to put a condom on a cucumber or a banana, it opens the door for them to have sexual conversations with one another. What do you expect? If you teach them how to use a condom and tell them, "All right, don't have sex, but if you do, here is what to do," it's like sending them to the mall with a credit card but telling them not to buy anything. Eventually that credit card is going to be used. Just like the condoms are going to be used after a while. The point is, you are taunting people to have sex.

So many companies profit from getting people to have sex. Look at the companies that sell pregnancy tests. They want as many people as possible to have sex. They would love it if every single person in the country were having sex all the time. They don't want anybody to teach abstinence as a way of life. They don't even want people to know the word *abstinence* exists. They don't want people to know you can wait and not have sex until after you're married. It works for me. It works for a lot of us. But you'd never know it from what you see on TV or at the magazine stand.

They've almost turned sex into a drug. Once you start, you're not going to be able to stop. They know that. They want you to be hooked. They want to take away any sense that it's shameful to have sex before marriage. We're sending kids out with a loaded gun these days. You talk about how to have safe sex. Kids are going to want to experiment. They always have and they always will. They are going to try the condom on with their boyfriend, or girlfriend, or anyone else who will try it. They are going to want to see what it feels like. You're giving them a false blanket, a plastic latex cover. But the world has many consequences for the actions you take. It's not all fun and games.

I wonder about the messages girls are getting, especially. Girls give sex for love, and guys give love for sex. But girls are sleeping with more guys now, and not because they want to but because they feel as if the guy is not going to love them the same or treat them the same if they don't sleep with him. They worry he'll break up with them. Girls need to know that it is admirable to wait until you get married. They need to know that it's okay to stick up for themselves.

Guys want to marry a nice, sweet girl who maybe has not had sex. They want someone they can take home to Mom and Dad. They want somebody respectful. They don't want the kind of girl who has dropped her pants for every one of his buddies. I think girls are being fed a lie. Of course guys want to score. They want to have sex. They want to get as many as they can. But guys aren't held to the same standard. You don't hear too many guys being called a slut or a ho. If a guy gets it all the time, the mentality is usually "Atta boy," or "Man, that guy is a stud." A girl who gets it all the time is a slut, a ho, a hooker, a tramp. She's whatever you want to call her. Girls need to be taught the other side of that. Girls should be told that it's a good thing if they can say, "No, I've never slept with anybody. I've never found anybody whom I liked that much, and, quite frankly, I'm worth waiting for." Girls aren't taught that now. Girls now are dropping to the peer pressure of having sex because they assume they can find love that way. This is sad and really unfortunate.

Parents need to talk to their kids. Most parents assume their kids are having sex. So what do they do? They go to the doctor and get them on birth control so they won't embarrass the family. Or they get them on birth control and say it's to make their daughters "more regular." They hand out birth control like candy. Well, doctors get kickbacks for handing out birth control, and parents feel better because they may not get embarrassed by their daughter getting pregnant. But hold on here. Instead of making it easier for your kids to have sex, why not sit them down for a serious talk? Why not say, "I know nowadays most kids are having sex. However, here's what you need to know: It's okay to be a virgin. That is the only safe sex there is. If you're going to have sex, let us know and we will put you on the pill. But there are consequences to your actions, and we are not talking about parental consequences."

Girls need to be taught that they can say no. Guys need to understand that they can be told no. What woman wants to marry a man who's been sleeping around his whole life? I don't know any. Most girls would much rather marry a virgin than marry a guy who has been hooking it up for the last ten years. Who can blame them? How can a guy like that be faithful? I mean, if you let a guy sleep around for five or ten years, and he's having sex and casual flings that are not even what you would call a relationship, how is he going to decide all of a sudden that he's only going to sleep with one person for the rest of his life? Somebody needs to talk to guys and say, "Look, it may be fun now, but it's going to be a hard habit to break. If you're sleeping around, it's going to be really hard for you to be faithful to your wife."

If we keep teaching and selling so-called safe sex, we are going to end up like Africa one day. We are going to have rampant HIV and AIDS and rampant rates of kids being born out of wedlock. Look at our divorce rate right now. Nobody talks about the divorce rate on TV because that is not a fun or exciting subject. That's not a reality people want to hear about. We are in a downward spiral in this country with sex and with marriage. Eventually people are never going to get married, or when they do, they are just going to get married for a couple of years. Too many people treat divorce casually. You hear about people who have been divorced three or four times by the time they are forty or forty-five and people consider that normal. It blows my mind.

Somebody needs to have the guts to talk about this. I really think it's up to parents to have the forethought to say, "One day it's going to catch up to you." Most parents don't feel comfortable talking with their kids about sex. Well, if you don't talk to them about it, they are going to find out from somebody else. Somebody else is going to try to push sex on them. I'd much rather have my parents tell me about it than MTV or Cinemax or HBO. I think parents need to say, "Look, even if you have had sex, you still can stop, you can wait, you can not have sex, you can say from this day forward I am not going to, I am going to wait until I get married."

People are not being taught about the massive bag of emotions that comes along with sex. The school systems need to teach kids about the emotional side, too. You wouldn't even know there is an emotional side to sex from watching TV. You wouldn't know it from the sex-ed classes you get in school. People have tried to take the emotions out of it and almost make it animalistic. They want to make it as if it's just two creatures that have hormones they can't suppress, and if it feels good, do it. Sex is not special anymore.

We have become a society where people feel there are no consequences to their actions. Have a good time. Live it up. Be with as many people as you want. It's time for parents to stop being embarrassed and stop trying to be their kids' friends and stop trying to be cool. It's time for them to tell their kids, "We're going to talk about sex, okay? If you feel uncomfortable, I'm sorry, but this is what you need to know. There is an emotional side to it. There are consequences to your actions."

People have been fooled into accepting this idea that sex is like test-driving a car before you buy it. That's how they look at marriage. It's like they get married because they've found the best person to have sex with. But if it's all about who is the best in bed, then eventually you're going to wonder who else might be out there. Is there someone else who would be better? That's not what marriage is about. That's not even what sex is about. But as long as people are encouraged to see sex that way, they are never going to be satisfied.

You don't get married because you want to have sex with somebody. You want to marry somebody because you want to experience sex with that person and keep it special between the two of you. People get married because they think, All right, he's the best lover I've had, so I'll stay with him. But that's going to wear off. People don't look the same when they are older. There has to be more to marriage than sex. They don't look at the best-friend side of it. The side that says, "I truly love and care about this person." Now people are getting married because they think it's the best sex they've found, or they don't want other people to have sex with that person. But basing marriage on sex is a recipe for divorce.

I think we've all seen examples of this. You see people who truly love each other who somehow can't stay faithful. Why is that? They say it's because they are not being satisfied in the bedroom. Is that because you're not being satisfied physically, or is it because you're emotionally not connected to the person because you were never really connected in the first place? If you never had that connection to start off, you don't know how special it can be. And one day you're going to get bored. That's why you see so many people getting divorced. They're bored. It's that simple. People fall into this trap of ignoring their emotional needs and looking to satisfy their sexual drive in some new way all the time. They think the only way they can be satisfied is by trying new things, jumping on different people, and getting their heart going.

I see a lot of this in young people. Once they have sex, they think they should be having sex all the time. They think that if they don't like it, then they are doing something wrong. Maybe someone doesn't enjoy it because they don't really want to be having sex. But they have been given this message telling them, "If you don't like it, you're doing something wrong. So go practice because practice makes perfect. Get better at it, and then you'll be a pro." Well, maybe if you're crying or you don't want to do it and you're being pressured into it, it's not going to be fun. Eventually, if you do it over and over again, you're going to become numb to it. Where does that leave you? You're going to be trying to find this gratification, and you may never be able to find it because you're so numb to the idea of intimacy in the bedroom.

That is why I have decided to stay a virgin, because, luckily, people who influence my life came to me and told me the reality of sex. They taught me responsibility. Now you see so many deadbeat dads because nobody told them they had to be responsible. If you get a girl pregnant, tough luck for the girl. It's all the girl's problem. A guy can run away, still have his life, and sleep around. If you don't teach people responsibility, what do you expect?

I've talked to a lot of people about this. I've asked them, "Why are you a virgin?" Or, "Why not?" Nine times out of ten, they didn't know what they were getting into with sex. They felt they had to have sex. You know, something like, "Oh, well, it's time because we've been together this long." People have not been taught to consider the consequences, or the patterns, so they don't give any real thought to any of that. Too many people have never learned values.

My decision to stay a virgin was really pretty simple. I realized that sex is far more than something to make me feel good on the inside. Sure, it feels good in the sexual sense, but what about the mental sense? There is an emotional attachment there, and there are a lot of things that can go wrong. Ask yourself, "Do I love somebody enough that I would be willing to have a kid with her?" Most people don't look at it that way. Too many see sex as being only about personal gratification. But I think abstinence is cool, or it should be, anyway. People need to change their mode of thinking. They need to be able to stand up and be proud of being a virgin, the way I am. That's what I say to people: "Look, I'm a virgin. If you're not, great, but I am, and I'm proud of it just like you're proud of hooking up with twelve people."

CHAPTER 14

Give Kids the Vote

We can all agree we have a huge problem with voter apathy. Most people don't care enough to vote. Even most of those who do vote barely pay any attention to the candidates and their positions. Something drastic has to be done. We have to find some way to shake up the political process and force politicians to connect with the voting public, especially younger voters, in a less superficial way. I have the perfect idea: Let's lower the voting age to sixteen.

If that sounds crazy to you, maybe you haven't studied your history closely enough. It was only thirty-three years ago when the twenty-sixth Amendment to the United States Constitution was ratified, lowering the national voting age from twenty-one to eighteen. That move was attacked in some quarters at the time as dangerous and misguided, but it has worked out just fine. Now young people in the United States and in several other countries around the world are pushing hard for their rights.

The city council in Cambridge, Massachusetts, voted in early 2002 to give seventeen-year-olds the right to vote, but the proposed law change ended up getting stuck in the state legislature. Last September, voters as young as sixteen and seventeen were allowed to vote in a mayoral primary in Baltimore, Maryland, because the general election was scheduled for fourteen months later and anyone eligible for the general election had the right to vote in the primary. State representatives in Maine, Texas, and California have considered introducing new legislation to lower the voting age to seventeen in each of those states. The British Parliament has debated lowering the voting age in Great Britain from eighteen to sixteen, and in Germany, there has even been consideration of lowering the voting age all the way down to twelve.

Before we go any further, please spare me any wisecracks about teenagers being uninformed. Granted, many don't know as much as they could about current events, but that's true of everyone in this country. Maybe if we show some respect for the young, we can engage them in the political process at a time when they are full of ideas and imagination. Maybe we can make politics interesting and exciting to them, instead of a tired duty to be performed every so often with all the joy and enthusiasm of changing the oil on your lawn mower or taking the dog outside so it can do its business.

The important thing is to think in terms of patterns. We need to establish new patterns of voter behavior. To do that, we have to look at the small window of opportunity that opens before the excitement of voting for the first few times gives way to numbing disillusionment. If we give sixteen-year-olds the vote, they will actually be voting for the first time at an age where they are much more likely to become engaged in that experience. They are much more likely to become regular voters, instead of getting bored and caught up in other things.

Think about it. If you're sixteen, you're probably still living with your parents, and your parents are probably talking politics. What better way for a young person to develop an interest in politics than starting to vote at an age when his parents are there for him? Sure, not every parent is going to want to talk politics with a teenager. But I guarantee many will. And let's face it, you don't have that much going on in your life at that age, so you're probably going to go vote. What does every sixteen-year-old want? To feel that he or she is taking one step closer to adulthood. To be respected and seen as grown up. The responsibility of voting fits in great with that. A lot of sixteen-year-olds have jobs. They are old enough to pay taxes to the government, but they aren't old enough to have a say in how that money is spent? That's just not right.

Voting is a responsibility, but it's also a right. One of the foundations of our democracy has always been the idea that if we as citizens met our responsibilities, we were entitled to certain rights. The hot-button issue has always been taxes. Is it fair to tax people without letting them participate in democracy? The Bostonians who gathered on the night of December 16, 1773, didn't think so. They were ticked off because the British Parliament in London had started taxing tea being unloaded in the harbor. They said they couldn't accept "taxation without representation." So they dumped more than three hundred chests full of tea into Boston Harbor. The so-called Boston Tea Party was a big step toward our independence as a country, and it's amazing that the basic concept behind that protest gets forgotten so often.

We need to redefine how we think of young people. That's the first step to redefining how people in general think of politics. I hear a lot of people say that lowering the voting age would be ridiculous. They point to statistics that show that eighteen-year-olds vote in smaller numbers than other age groups. But so what? The question isn't how many are voting now, but how come more aren't voting? Eighteen-year-olds have never been taught or encouraged to vote in mass numbers, and that's why they don't. They have never gotten into the routine of voting. Most eighteen-year-olds are dealing with a lot of change in their lives. They've moved out of their parent's house or they are in college, so it's harder to vote. Usually if you're in college, that's a different voting district, so you need to re-register or get an absentee ballot. That's a hassle. So even if you've registered to vote back home, there's a good chance you won't actually make it to the voting booth.

But flash back two years earlier. Say you're sixteen and living at home. Say your parents start talking about politics with you months or even years before you are legally entitled to vote at sixteen. Maybe you even watch the Sunday talk shows together or the nightly news. You're around parents who consider voting important. Your parents are in the habit of voting. They can take you along with them to the polling place. You can sit down to dinner after you've all voted and talk about the election and what's at stake.

That is the way for young people to start to understand the importance of it. That is the way for young people to develop the feeling that they matter. People have forgotten that they have a responsibility to their nation to let their voices be heard. They have a responsibility to put their support behind the candidate they think is best for the job. They have a responsibility to pay attention and find out what's going on and what it means. It's just a question of learning that lesson early. You can make a lifelong habit of voting. You can get in the routine of realizing that you can be heard and that you're not just a nobody.

We should also make it easier for people to register to vote. If the voting age was sixteen, the same as when people are eligible to get their driver's licenses, you could put the two together: Anyone who gets a license is automatically registered to vote. A lot more people will be voting that way. As it is now, you're eligible to vote at eighteen, but a lot of people don't even take the time to register when they turn eighteen. It doesn't seem worth going out of their way to do. But if you can knock out two things at once, people are going to start voting a lot more.

That could have some surprising benefits. More parents would vote, too. If your son or daughter starts asking you a lot of questions about politics and voting, you're going to want to have answers. You're going to want to sound informed. So you're going to do some homework and catch up on the issues and candidates. A lot of parents would get more involved because they want their kids to get more involved. They want to set a good example. It goes back to my point that by showing respect for young people, you're generating more interest in voting. Young people are enthusiastic and curious. That enthusiasm can rub off on others.

Let's look at the arguments on the other side. What are they? That's a good question. The main argument against giving sixteen-year-olds the vote seems to be that it doesn't make sense because eighteen-year-olds don't vote in large numbers, so why should we let sixteen-year-olds vote? How stupid is that? If you're saying it's a bad thing that more eighteen-year-olds aren't voting, that means you would like to see more participation, not less. So why not give sixteen-year-olds the vote? What could it hurt? Why not give them the option? If I'm wrong and only small numbers of sixteen-year-olds take advantage of the opportunity, then where's the problem? At least we are encouraging politicians to look beyond their narrow interest groups and attack advertising.

You know what I think? I think politicians are flat-out scared. They worry about young people voting in large numbers and having their say. That's terrifying to a lot of politicians. They wouldn't just be able to rely on their consultants to tell them how to pull the same political tricks candidates always pull. They might have to find a way to show some freshness and energy in their thinking. They might have to talk to young people and really listen to what they have to say. They might have to take some chances and try not to be so boring all the time. Do you think any sixteen-year-old would ever in a million years have voted for someone like Gray Davis? No way. They see a phony, pompous, blow-dried candidate like that on TV, and they know right away: "This guy sucks, we don't like him, he's terrible."

A lot of polling places are at high schools. Good grief, think how many students would vote if they could just take a quick break from their class and go over and cast a vote, all without leaving their school. That prospect has politicians nervous, and I say anything that makes politicians look over their shoulders has to be worth considering.

Young people are bright and smart. Politicians would have a harder time fooling them. It's easier for them to target an older demographic. They don't want to have to worry about alienating young people. They don't want to have to worry about keeping young people happy, because they know that when young people aren't happy, they are going to demand change.

People tend to forget how important young people are to the economy. Young people spend money like it's going out of style. They are the ones keeping the shops open during recessions. They are the ones buying the video games and buying the new TVs and buying the new cars and buying the new stereo equipment. They are the ones buying tickets to movies on the weekends. They are supporting this economy by a massive amount of tax dollars. So why not let them have the option of voting?

We let eighteen-year-olds fly a high-performance jet in wartime, or we give them an M-16 and send them off to a distant country and tell them to start shooting people. Voting is not nearly as big a deal as fighting for your country. If you can start fighting at age eighteen, to me it totally makes sense for you to start learning about voting and the responsibility of choosing our leaders before that. It takes time to learn that responsibility. Lawmakers think sixteen-year-olds are responsible enough to drive, and a car can be a deadly weapon. More kids die in car wrecks each year than die from drugs or alcohol. So if you think a kid is responsible enough to drive by himself at sixteen, then he's certainly responsible enough to vote.

We need to teach kids that dreams can happen. We need to let them now that we don't see them as a bunch of idiots. Come on, look at how the media portrays young people. They're stupid. They're morons. They're screwups. They're druggies. They're drunks. They're party animals. Well, if you want to work to change that, give kids more responsibility and let their voices be heard. Let them know they're wrong to think of Generations X and Y as generations of screwups.

You'd be surprised how much the mentality of young people can be changed. Young people have a hunger to know who they are. They have a deep desire to know their place in society. If you can send a strong message to a young person early on that he has a place in society, and his voice can be heard, that can have a huge effect. If you can let kids know that they do matter, that their votes matter and people will listen to them, you'd be amazed how much the mind-set of young people would change. Too often now you hear young people saying things like, "Oh, screw politics," or "I hate it, it's stupid. I don't understand it, and I don't care."

If you want kids to care enough to understand politics, and how the world works, and taxes and finances and everything else, let them start to vote. They'll study those issues. They'll look at it as a privilege, something of importance. I know so many kids who never voted in college because they went off to school and never registered to vote. They didn't have a chance to register when they were sixteen and to develop a routine and learn to take it seriously. Instead they fell into the habit of figuring that they'd start voting down the road. If you want people in this country to stop voting, you're doing a good job of it. We're in real danger of seeing voter turnout continue to drop year by year, and election by election, because we're losing young people. We're losing the people who might really have passion and fresh energy.

Old people tend to become passive and set in their ways. That's just human nature. But young people don't. They don't have time for that. They haven't learned that yet. They might try to look cool, but inside, they care about things. A lot of the time they care too much. But that's great when it comes to politics. We're talking about a whole source of creative energy we have yet to tap.

If a young person gets involved in politics and finds a candidate worth supporting, there is a good chance he will go out to campaign for that candidate. They don't have a forty-hour-a-week job. They don't have tee times locking them into eighteen holes. They have extra time, so why not put them to work and get them out there campaigning? They are the ones who can make phone calls, put up yard signs, and go stand on the street corners handing out flyers. Why would you not want to use them? They are a terrific tool.

Sure, maybe sometimes they are innocent. Maybe they are even somewhat naive. Great. They haven't learned to think that they have all the answers. They haven't learned to run on autopilot and forget that politics in the end is about connecting with people. Sixteen-year-olds and seventeen-year-olds can be a great tool to use in a political race. And best of all, if you get them involved when they are young, you are going to establish a pattern of voting and involvement in politics that can last a lifetime. That is the way to create leaders for the future. That is the way to energize future generations.

More than anything, giving sixteen-year-olds the right to vote is a way to teach them responsibility. We have an epidemic of irresponsibility in this country. No one is ever to blame for anything. There is always some excuse, or explanation, or lawyerly twist to tell us why this or that person should not be held responsible for something they've done or not done. We're sending the message to young people that nothing they do has any real consequences. We don't listen to the young. We don't trust the young. We don't respect the young.

Politicians are basically teaching young people that their vote doesn't matter, because they are not mature enough and their ideas are unimportant. Well, if you're teaching a generation that their ideas don't matter until they are eighteen, or twenty-two or twenty-three, they are going to act as if they don't matter. They are going to act as if their decisions don't matter. They are going to act as if there are no consequences to their actions, and they are going to act as if they don't care. Give them the opportunity to feel that they do matter, and they will act as if they care.

You don't teach kids to read and write when they are twelve years old. Or fifteen. That would be crazy. No, you start them young. Reading and writing are so important, you want them to have some time to learn them well. It should be the same with politics. It should be the same with learning about democracy and how the world works. We should start them young. We teach them in school about government and current events and social studies, but that's a hollow exercise unless we show it's not all just words. It's much more than that. It's choosing the direction of this country. It's choosing the kind of leaders we want. It's choosing who we are, and who we want to be.

At sixteen you're old enough to vote. You're competent enough to think for yourself and not just follow the lead of your parents. You're old enough to have your own ideas and thoughts about the world. So why not let young people vote?

CHAPTER 15

You Gotta Serve Somebody

Anybody who has listened to my radio show knows how much I love my country. It makes me smile, just thinking about what a great country this is. But I'd like to see some fundamental changes. I'd like Americans to be less selfish, less focused on themselves, and more aware of others. That's why I want to see national service for everyone.

Let's face it: Americans are obsessed with themselves. Everything is me, myself, and I. No one else matters. People fall into this attitude that as long as I have the newest car, and the best clothes, and the best friends, that's all that matters. Kids nowadays will do anything to be popular. They worry about the littlest things, the most meaningless things. But I guarantee that would be different if kids see what other people have to deal with day in and day out.

We need to do something about this incredible selfishness, and that means changing how people are taught. My generation has been taught to think of ourselves all the time. We want to do something for others only if the task is easy and painless. We're full of pride. We want to be better than everyone else. We don't want to help others because it may not get us that new Beemer quite as fast, or we may not get that new house quite as fast. We are so quick to play the victim card, even when it comes to the luxuries we feel we deserve, instead of helping others.

Doing the right thing is much more fulfilling than driving a new car. Freeing another person from suffering or hardship is much more admirable and gratifying than having an extra $5,000 in your stock portfolio. But if you're not exposed to the idea of helping others when you are at an impressionable age, it's easy to fall into thinking you're the only one who matters. Being an American is an amazing blessing. We're so lucky. But living the American dream is not just chasing your own dream. It's also helping others live their dream. That's what we have lost in this country.

Americans used to know what it meant to serve their country. That was part of what it meant to be an American. You served your country when it needed your help. I think that mind-set came from seeing people pitch in so often during hard times to make things better for the community. Just look at the Great Depression. The Depression taught people to depend on their neighbors. Look at World War I and World War II. Hard times brought people together during those circumstances as well. No one was too good to pitch in and get their hands dirty. Those times changed Americans' hearts and minds. They taught people how to put others first.

My grandfather served in World War II and never questioned that responsibility. To him, that was part of being a citizen of the United States. You took the good with the bad; you did your duty without a lot of complaining. He was sent abroad and didn't see my grandmother for almost three years. Many of the men he served with came home to three-year-olds they were seeing for the first time. Men like my grandfather witnessed terrible things happening all around them, but they knew it was worth it to fight against dictators and to fight for freedom.

We have changed so much over the last sixty years. Back then we were a society in which women watched their husbands leave home to serve overseas, knowing they might be seeing their husbands for the last time, because they might give their lives to save others. Many of those same women were willing to go to work, doing the heavy lifting in greasy, dirty machine shops. They didn't have to do that. But they knew they were part of something larger than themselves. They wanted to contribute to the war effort, not only so their husbands and brothers and sons and nephews could come home sooner but also so their cause would carry the day.

Nowadays, most Americans don't really believe in anything, except themselves. That's why so many are so miserable. We should be the happiest country in the world by far, if you think about it. We're safer than anyone else. We have better technology than anyone else. We have a wonderful government. We have the freedom to say what we want to say when we want to say it. We have the freedom to read what we want to read. We have the freedom to write what we want to write. We have the freedom to pray to whomever we want. But a lot of people don't even begin to understand how good we have it. They take our way of life for granted. They have never helped anybody else, or served anybody else, and that's a problem not just for them but for all of us.

Look at the executives in this country who are paid hundreds of millions of dollars a year and for some reason are not happy. That's a sad thing. These executives lose all perspective. They start thinking things like, I have $120 million, but that guy over there has $122 million, and I want to have $122 million, too, so I better go talk to him and try to figure out how he does it. They can't even spend the money they already have, but they're more worried about how they compare to other executives than anything else. They're not willing to put their families first, let alone getting out in the community and really helping someone else with some of that money. These executives get so money-hungry, so narrow-minded, all they can think about is buying that new car or that new condo in the Hamptons or that new house on Maui. Self-gratification is all that matters.

Or look at how outrageous the violent crime rate is. People like Michael Moore try to blame it on guns. That was what *Bowling for Columbine* was all about. But the problem is people, not the weapons themselves. The bigger problem is the way that so many people have become so focused on themselves, they can cook up a justification for just about anything. Seriously. These people will do whatever it takes to get people out of their lives if they think they're somehow standing in the way of their happiness. They might steal from them. They might even kill them.

Lawmakers should ask themselves, "Okay, what's going on? Why are we so selfish?" It's because we are being taught to be selfish. We're being taught to get whatever we can get, whatever it costs, and screw anybody in our path. If we truly want America to continue to be the greatest country in the world, we have to be bold enough to do something about this epidemic of selfishness. We need to have the courage to make some major changes, no matter how much people might complain at first about actually having to think about someone besides themselves.

We need to make community service an integral part of education. Let's say you start in the third or fourth grade, and from then on community service would be required of all students until they graduate from high school. Think of what a difference that could make. Reaching kids when they are at a young, impressionable age is the best way to make sure they see themselves as part of the wider world out there. It is the best way to snap so many young people out of this trap of thinking it's all about having money and looking good and being cool, or thinking that the biggest problems anyone could have are worrying about grades or who to ask to the prom. If you start kids out doing community service when they are young, they will be more likely to appreciate what they have.

You could put students out in the community dealing with people who are underprivileged. Some would be in hospitals working with people who are sick. Some would be with the elderly, helping them spend their declining years in dignity. Some would be helping out in a soup kitchen, serving up meal after meal after meal to a seemingly unending line of people. Some would be in the projects, working with people there.

Talk about changing the value of an education. Now kids are dropping out because it's not cool to go to school. Well, go take a good, long look at life in the projects, where you could possibly end up if you don't get an education, and that will change their mentality. Maybe that will encourage you to think, Okay, I am blessed to have this opportunity, I am blessed that I have parents who work and provide for me, instead of always feeling as if you deserve a free ride. Maybe it will inspire you to make the most of this free education, instead of worrying about that new car you want or about being popular. Maybe it will remind you of all you have to be thankful about: youth and freedom and the ability to play sports and the chance to do whatever you want to do.

If students were required to perform a certain amount of community service each week, they could make a difference in other peoples' lives, and they could also learn to see their own lives differently. There would be no way to avoid it. If you are out there in the community, helping someone who is fighting every day to beat cancer and stay alive, that is going to change your mentality. That experience is going to make you less likely to whine about not being able to buy the new pair of shoes you want or the new coat. I truly believe that we could make people less hateful toward others. If you put service into education, you could change the infrastructure of the American mind-set in a single generation. That would be a pretty amazing thing. You would see violence go down. You would see happiness go up.

Some of what young people gain from that experience could stay with them their entire lives. They could get some good advice from these people they meet from other backgrounds and other life experiences. It might be an old person, or someone in jail, or someone fighting for her life in a hospital. But if you put in an average of seventy hours of community service each year you are in school, from the third grade onward, there is a very good chance that someone you meet is going to make a major impact on your life. Somebody is going to influence you and might possibly change the way your life turns out.

That kind of influence can take some time to kick in, too. You might hear a voice inside your head for years, half forgetting the person behind the voice. Something like that happened to Mitch Albom, that sportswriter in Detroit. He always thought about his old teacher, Morrie Schwartz, even as he was living his life in a way that was at odds with a lot of what Morrie had taught him. Then when Morrie was dying of cancer, Albom decided to visit him a few times, and he ended up writing a book, *Tuesdays with Morrie,* that was on the *New York Times* best-seller list for years. The book's popularity showed that a lot of people understand the importance of reaching out to others and looking for the best in them and the best in ourselves.

Morrie told Albom:

People are only mean when they're threatened, and that's what our culture does. That's what our economy does. Even people who have jobs in our economy are threatened, because they worry about losing them. And when you get threatened, you start looking out only for yourself. You start making money a god. It is all part of this culture. . . .

Look, no matter where you live, the biggest defect we human beings have is our shortsightedness. We don't see what we could be. We should be looking at our potential, stretching ourselves into everything we can become. But if you're surrounded by people who say "I want mine now," you end up with a few people with everything. . . . The problem, Mitch, is that we don't believe we are as much alike as we are. Whites and blacks, Catholics and Protestants, men and women. If we saw each other as more alike, we might be very eager to join in one big human family in this world, and to care about that family the way we care about our own.

It's fine that as a nation we have a survival-of-the-fittest mentality, but we also have to keep in mind that everyone has a responsibility to his community. We have to take care of other people, even people we don't know. I'm not talking about socialism. I'm talking about being a caring nation. We need to get back to our roots, and you have to start with young, impressionable minds. There are things that kids need to learn through community service that can't be taught out of a textbook and can't be learned by listening to a speech from a teacher. They're real-life experiences.

We take a lot of pride in being number one as a country, but there are no guarantees it will always be that way. Other countries are catching up to us. One reason for that is that in a lot of other countries, young people have to serve their country for a year or two. People complain, of course, but most do their duty. Some serve in the military, but many work in hospitals or drive old people to their hospital visits or bring meals to old people in their homes. They also serve abroad, helping people in other countries to learn basic skills or working with them to develop programs and infrastructure so they can help themselves.

We could make serving abroad an option for students, too. Instead of doing a couple of hours of service a week, they could be part of a program for young people spending the summer in a foreign country, helping people there. When President Kennedy said, "Ask not what your country can do for you, ask what you can do for your country," he was articulating one of the foundations of our democracy. The Peace Corps hasn't always known what it wanted to be, and sometimes it's hard to know whether people volunteer mostly as a way to broaden themselves and have stories to tell when they get back home or whether they really take service seriously. We need to think about ways to continue to update the Peace Corps and to use it to help people in other countries improve their economy.

That might sound like a paradox. If we're helping other countries strengthen their economies, wouldn't that hurt our competitive position? The answer is, yes and no. The most important thing is that we encourage our own people to think in terms of helping others, starting when they are young, and also in terms of broadening themselves through service. That holds true internationally, too. The world has become a very complex and confusing place, and we need every advantage we can find to help understand how other countries see us and what they want for themselves in the future.

The idea of service is as old as the Bible and as basic as faith. I'm not saying that every third-grader or every high-school student who takes part in community service has to see that work as an expression of faith, not at all. There's no need to mention faith in that context. But for a lot of us, the two are connected. Faith makes us want to be better people, and that makes us want to work to help others, too. President Bush talked about that at a National Prayer Breakfast in February 2001.

"Faith remains important to the compassion of our nation," the president said that morning. "Millions of Americans serve their neighbor because they love their God. Their lives are characterized by kindness and patience, and service to others. They do for others what no government really can ever do—no government program can really ever do: They provide love for another human being. They provide hope even when hope comes hard."

It all starts with respect. You want violence to go down in this country? Don't get rid of guns. Start with kids learning to respect other people and to appreciate what they do have instead of wanting what they don't have. That's how you turn this country around. That's how you change generations. That's how you change mind-sets. That's how you keep America truly the greatest country in the world.

CHAPTER 16

NASCAR, the Next Big Thing

If there's a sport out there that takes as much abuse as NASCAR, I'd like to know what it is. Heck, even synchronized swimming—you know, with the nose plugs and all—has become almost respected. But for some reason, NASCAR still gets mocked. That's probably because people write it off as a redneck sport. I have to admit, when I was younger, I used to think you went to see a NASCAR race only if you were a redneck. Then one weekend I checked out the Bristol Motor Speedway in Bristol, Tennessee, and everything changed. What can I say? I fell in love. Now I know why NASCAR is the fastest-growing sport in America and why it's on the verge of really hitting the big time.

Team executives in the major sports leagues are always talking about how fan-friendly they are, but they've got to be kidding. NASCAR is as fan-friendly as it gets. Heck, they even let you bring in your own cooler. You buy one seat for the weekend, and sure, prices have gone up in recent years, but compared to football or basketball or even baseball, it's still a good deal. These days you practically have to be rich to take a family of four to most professional sporting events. Just buying hot dogs and popcorn and Cokes and a souvenir will set you back more than a hundred bucks. Everyone complains about the high prices, and that has alienated a lot of fans. It takes the fun out of those sports.

NASCAR is a family sport all the way. You take your wife and kids to the racetrack and spend the whole weekend together. That's time you're going to remember, not like going to watch some big, splashy movie with a lot of dumb special effects or playing miniature golf. NASCAR has always been about family. The man who founded the National Association for Stock Car Auto Racing in Daytona Beach, Florida, back in 1948, Big Bill France, passed on the leadership to his son, Bill France Jr., in 1972, and then last year, the grandson, Brian France, took over as chairman of the board. I'd call that keeping it in the family. Big Bill took what was pretty much an excuse to get together some fast cars and some good ole boys used to running moonshine, just to see what would happen. The France family had vision, and they were in it for the long haul. But NASCAR would never have become the NASCAR we know today if doing right by the family tradition was not so important to Big Bill and his sons and grandsons.

Look at all the great drivers whose fathers were great drivers before them. Obviously you have to start with Dale Earnhardt Jr., whose father, Dale Earnhardt Sr., died in that famous crash in early 2001. Maybe the greatest racing family ever was the Pettys. Richard Petty grew up in Level Cross, North Carolina, and he used to go watch his dad, Lee Petty, race on weekends on his way to three Grand National championships and a victory in the first-ever Daytona 500. Richard went on to become the king of NASCAR, finishing his career with a total of two hundred victories, far more than any other driver. Richard's son Kyle followed the family tradition, and his son Adam was a NASCAR driver until his tragic death in 2000 at age nineteen. Bobby Allison and his son Davey finished first and second in the 1988 Daytona 500. You also have the Fittipaldis. And the Andrettis. The sport gets passed on from generation to generation because the whole environment is so much geared toward families and family values.

You can pull your camper up and set yourself up and be ready to take in a long weekend of action and entertainment. That's why it's such a bonding experience, because there is so much to talk about from the start of the event to the finish and so much time to talk about it. If you're really a fan, you get there early enough to show up Thursday morning at five A.M. or so when the first of the race cars are unloaded from transport trucks onto the speedway. A carnival atmosphere takes over. More than one hundred thousand people mill around, telling stories about great races they've seen. Once you've been part of a racing weekend, you'll never forget it.

Every second counts. No one wants to miss an instant of action when the cars are out there barreling along at close to two hundred miles per hour. Anything can happen, and everyone knows it. That's what outsiders don't get. The people missing out on the thrill of NASCAR just haven't had the adrenaline rush of hearing these great machines roaring around the speedway and knowing that one false move can have disastrous consequences. Heck, watching a baseball game, you can go wait in line for beers and if you miss an inning or two, so what? Basketball is even worse. You can doze through the whole regular season and not miss anything important, since everyone knows the season doesn't really get going for real until the playoffs start. Any NASCAR driver who makes it through another race has accomplished something. He has dodged a bullet. No other sport can match that level of intensity.

So much is riding on the possibility of one lapse. If a driver makes even a small mistake, he winds up crashing into a wall or maybe he sends someone else crashing into a wall. Look at the way America responded to the death of Dale Earnhardt. Now, part of that was just because of the way he handled himself. He was such a gutsy, aggressive driver. He would squeeze through a gap even if it meant banging up his fender or the fender of another driver. No problem. But his death triggered an emotional reaction across the country because it was so dramatic, too. People could connect with the drama of a man one minute being on top of the world, a champion race-car driver, and then, almost as fast as you could snap your fingers, it was all over. Bad luck was what took Earnhardt from us. He hit the wall at 160 miles per hour and his seat belt failed. That left him vulnerable to a fatal head injury. Earnhardt was just a totally fearless guy and a great, great driver. If an accident could take him, an accident can take anyone. Everyone who loves NASCAR has that feeling that heartache is always just around the corner, and that helps explain why people get so passionate about the sport.

People relate to race-car drivers. We all drive, first of all, or most of us anyway. And most of us drive too fast sometimes. It's fun. It feels good. It's exciting. It's every guy's dream. Every guy I know has always wanted to drive fast. They've always wanted to race and to get in their new cars and drive around fast with their buddies to show off. Back in high school, we all knew guys who spent all their time tinkering with cars and who wanted nothing more than to go a few miles an hour faster. The noisier their cars were, the better. They wanted you to look. They wanted to make a spectacle of themselves and their souped-up cars. That's basically the story of NASCAR, which started out as a bunch of crazy guys going nuts on dirt tracks in small towns out in the country. This was just after World War II, and even drivers who had never been moonshiners tried to drive like them. There was an old TV show called the *Dukes of Hazzard*. That was pretty much what we were talking about. Those guys were a little more reckless, a little more hell-bent on getting their kicks, and they drove fast cars and wanted to race all the time.

But racing has changed over the years. It's so sophisticated now. If you think about it, most football fans have at least tossed the pigskin around in their backyard a few times. Most baseball fans played at least a couple years of Little League, and maybe they still play on the company

softball team, beer bellies and all. People have kicked around a soccer ball and shot a basketball. But no one except the professionals has had the feeling of strapping himself into a souped-up race car and taking a spin around an oval track. That's an entirely different realm of experience, like being a jet-fighter pilot or an astronaut. People love to watch NASCAR races because they's so dramatic and otherworldly.

It's a dream, but it's very down to earth, too. You can relate to all the people involved in putting a single race-car driver out there and all the hard work and sweat that go into getting ready for any given race. It's such a team effort. Everybody gets credit. The pit crew is a huge part of determining whether a driver will succeed or not. If a driver goes into pit row in sixth place and comes out in fourth place, that has nothing to do with the driver; it has everything to do with the guys who aren't making millions of dollars. These are real, everyday people. Anybody can learn how to change a tire fast. Anybody has a chance to do that job. Anybody has a chance to be a gas-can man. Anybody has a chance to be a mechanic. Anybody has a chance to duct tape a car. And all those jobs are superimportant. I'm telling you, you can be the greatest driver in the world and if somebody didn't get a lug nut on tight back there on the rear tire, you have lost the race.

The driver is just as important as the engine man, who is just as important as the guy who changes the tires or wipes the windshield or takes the duct tape off the front vent of the car. Everybody matters. And you don't have to go to school to be part of a pit crew. You don't have to be an amazing athlete who can jump six feet. You don't have to be seven feet tall or have three hundred pounds of muscle. You can be shaped like a blob and still be quick and efficient about gassing up a car. You don't drive the fancy car, but you're a member of the team. You belong, and you take pride in it, and there aren't any other sports where just anyone can get involved in that way.

Most sports are all about someone trying to prove how smart he is, but not NASCAR. Football fans are always talking about who the great-

est coach is and how brilliant he was to switch up defenses and keep blitzing or not blitzing or whatever. The media wants you to think that baseball is all about numbers, and comparing statistics, the way Bill James does in his work. The way these so-called expert commentators talk on TV, sometimes you'd think every move a manager makes is obvious ahead of time and that the actual players swinging the bat or throwing the pitch or diving to catch the ball are somehow beside the point. No one ever falls into that kind of thinking with NASCAR. Anyone can win on a given day, and it's all about who goes out there and does it. Strategy plays into that, of course, but still, it's basically about going out there and doing it. It's not about the predictions. Nobody ever predicts who is going to win a race. Why would they?

You see a guy go from last place, a lap down, and come back to win, and that's cool. Everyone can get behind that. It's so unpredictable, you have no clue. Other sports have been ruined because you can literally buy a championship. You can't buy a championship in NASCAR. Every man is equal. It's doesn't matter if you're fat or if you're slow. You get behind that wheel, and you're all equals. You have no guarantees. You know you are going to have your ups and downs. It's the same way a lot of people's everyday lives go. They have to show up at their jobs on time and work hard and perform.

NASCAR is a sport where people have to work hard just to make a paycheck. That's why we can relate to it. These spoiled athletes in other sports have it made. They sign these huge, multiyear deals for millions and millions of dollars, and they keep getting paid no matter what happens. They might have a lackluster year or several lackluster years. They might tear their ACL and sit out a year. But they always get paid. That's not how it is in the real world. If you have a lackluster month or two, you might get fired. Or if you screw up and come in late to work a couple of days in a row, you might get fired. In NASCAR, you put it on the line every week. If you don't perform well, you aren't going to win any money. You're only as good as your last race. If you come in last, nobody

is going to remember you. If you perform well and stay at the top of your game, you're going to be driving for a long time. You never heard about a guy getting a six-year contract or a ten-year contract in NASCAR. That's not how it works. You drive until you're not good anymore.

You have to like a sport without prima donnas. If you pay any attention to the NFL or the NBA, you'll get your fill of all the whining and complaining you hear from these pampered superstars. They ought to just shut up and play, and earn the piles of money they're getting, but instead it's constant bickering about which player can claim a team is his or about how so-and-so disrespected a player by not bowing down and kissing his feet. NASCAR is a prima donna–free zone. NASCAR is a bunch of good ole boys who go out there and give it their all week after week. You are going to drive the living crud out of that car until you either crash or win, and that's all there is to it.

That's why I think NASCAR is such an exciting sport and why it's grown. You can relate to these people, you can connect, unlike with those players of other sports that used to be great. You get with your buddies, and you all get a kick out of rooting for your guy who's hauling it around the track. You hope he wins. You can't connect with a guy like LeBron James, who is eighteen years old and already has a $100 million contract, and that's just from his sneaker company. You can't connect with a guy like Kobe Bryant. You can't connect with a Shaquille O'Neal. And those guys don't connect with their public. They don't make you feel as if you know them. You see them play more than a hundred games a year, and you don't even feel as if you know them.

You watch one NASCAR race and see the driver talk afterward, and you feel as if you know him. You feel as if you could talk to him, as if he's an actual person. It's kind of like after Brad Pitt and Jennifer Aniston were married, she noticed that strangers had a much easier time approaching her in public and talking to her than they did coming up to her husband. As part of the *Friends* cast, she was in their living room every single night. But Brad Pitt was on a movie set and up on the big screen.

He's a movie star. He wasn't in your living room. So people didn't have the feeling that they knew him, the way they did about Jennifer Aniston. That's a lot how it is with NASCAR. You have this basic, gut-level feeling that you know the drivers and all the people associated with the sport. And that's why I think it's such an addictive sport, because you really care what happens to these people.

Soccer is like that, too. It's a bunch of guys just running for ninety minutes, playing their hearts out to win. The guys are emotional, they get upset when they get cut off, they get very irritated, they bump, they grind, they get in between people. But when a basketball star has a bad game, he just says, "Oh well." He moves on and figures it doesn't matter much anyway because it's all about his contract and how much money he's made. Agents have ruined football and basketball because they convince these guys coming out of high school that they are worth $100 million, and then if they get only $80 million, they have a chip on their shoulder. They are angry and sulky because they feel disrespected, instead of appreciating how lucky they are to be living out a dream.

To the people who dismiss NASCAR because it's a redneck sport, I say: What's so bad about being a redneck? I think every one of us has a little redneck in us. It used to be that you never saw NASCAR being shown in a sports bar or at least not in a major city. It wasn't cool. But now you see it all over the place. NASCAR is still a redneck sport in a lot of ways, but at least it's honest about that. What's amazing is that NASCAR let NASCAR be what it is. It's a good-ole-boy sport. They didn't try to redefine the sport or cook up some focus group–tested new image. They found out what their niche market was and found out how to connect with them and build their success on that foundation of support.

No one is arguing that NASCAR is a showcase of diversity. It's a very white sport. Only one driver, Bill Lester, is black. That opens NASCAR up to all sorts of wild criticisms, including the charge from an associate of the Reverend Jesse Jackson in June 2003 that NASCAR represents "the last bastion of white supremacy" in American sports. The irony here is that NASCAR has been reaching out to Jackson after he put pressure on NASCAR at a 1999 conference. Jackson told the gathering, which included Bill France Jr.: "The fact of the matter is there is frustration because of exclusion. We must now turn that pain to power. We were qualified to play baseball before 1947. We are qualified to race cars now."

That was all it took to get the NASCAR leadership to agree to pony up $150,000 for Jackson's Rainbow/PUSH Coalition in 2001 and another $100,000 in 2002. I am sure they did this because they wanted to make Jackson go away. Sure, it shut him up for a while. But then his associate, Rainbow/PUSH board member Bill Shack, dropped the "white supremacy" bomb. And why not? Nobody would deny that Jackson is a smart man; so hey, he got hundreds of thousands out of NASCAR the first time, so why not roll the dice and try again?

But this time NASCAR fought back, asking Jackson why he hadn't used the money he received from NASCAR to help sponsor a black driver. Jackson ducked the question. But to this day, he still has not used that money to help a black driver break into the sport. What he did instead was to raise the heart rate of many Americans, black and white. What he did instead was push people toward a racist mind-set. Now everyone involved with NASCAR will automatically think the worst of Jackson. They think he's a liar who just wants to stir up racism. And can you blame them? NASCAR gave Jackson money, thinking he was going to help minorities get into racing, and instead he lined his pockets with cash and walked away. He wasn't really interested in doing something to address the shortage of black drivers, because he wasn't interested in NASCAR or even in sports in general. He's interested only in stoking controversy whenever and wherever he can. If Jesse Jackson wants me to feel guilty because there are not more black faces at NASCAR events, well, I'm sorry, but no one is telling you not to come. This is not an elite sport that only the rich can afford. NASCAR is open to everyone who is interested.

The change in sponsorship earlier this year could have a major impact on how NASCAR is seen across the country, outside of the South. RJ Reynolds Tobacco had been sponsoring the Winston Cup series for thirty-two years, paying about $45 million a year, but now car racing has a telecommunications giant behind it. Nextel is paying $40 million a year to put its name on the event and will throw in another $30 million a year to promote NASCAR. It's always hard to predict how a sport will grow, but any NASCAR lover has to agree with me when I say more and more people are going to get hooked on the rush of car racing. The sport already has more than 60 million fans, and that number is going to increase dramatically.

You're going to see a lot of people changing their minds about NASCAR. People who didn't want to give it credit as a real sport are going to decide to give it a chance and realize all they've been missing. That's going to be very bad news for all the spoiled-brat millionaires who are doing their best to ruin our major team sports. They drive up in their Hummers, their SUVs, and their Mercedes. They live in their huge houses, and they have all these domestic violence disputes. They cheat on their wives all the time, the way Kobe did. Other sports are so worried about finding new ways to market themselves, but the lesson from NASCAR is: Be yourself. Let baseball be baseball. Let basketball be basketball. Don't keep throwing more money at these guys. If you pay them that much money, of course they are going to get greedy. Nobody should be paid $90 million to bounce a ball. That to me is ridiculous. Just you watch: Over the next few years, you are going to see other sports keep declining, and you're going to see NASCAR picking up cities and new racetracks and new fans, because people love it.

CHAPTER 17

What Boomers Didn't Learn about Family Values

The baby boomers have done their best to destroy the American family. A lot of them think they are wonderful parents, and they have a tall stack of self-help books and Laura Schlessinger books on tape that they will point to if you ask them to prove it, too. But what too many parents from the baby boom generation have forgotten is that family starts with family values. The key concept in family is "us," not "me." If you have devoted your life to looking out for me-me-me all the time, and you think you are being a good parent by trying to teach your kid how to look out for me-me-me all the time, well, you've missed the boat, my friend, and there is nothing I or anyone else can say to help you.

Just look at how many lives have been messed up by this mentality of always trying to be better than everyone else, always trying to be bigger and stronger and smarter and more accomplished. I am not saying the baby boomers invented that way of thinking. No way. But they sure act as if they invented it, and they sure did their best to make everyone think so, too. They have devoted their whole lives to the mentality that you have to succeed no matter what and do whatever it takes. I don't know where that comes from, I really don't, unless they think they weren't pushed enough when they were children.

Part of the problem is the value placed on appearances. Somehow a notion has taken root that there is a whole persona you have to adopt to impress people and convince them that you have the perfect family. You know what I am talking about. Just take a look at that pile of Christmas cards you received last December. Not to knock your friends and family, but come on! Why do people try so hard to convince us with their Christmas cards that they have a great, perfect family? Why do they care so much that you get the impression that they are all happy, happy, happy, with not a care or problem in the world? Why do they want to look like *Little House on the Prairie* brought to the new modern world?

I wish I knew. But I truly do not. All I can say for sure is these parents who worry so much about having the perfect American family are the ones who push their kids like crazy but don't really parent their kids. It's one thing to push somebody to be successful. Anyone can do that. You don't even have to know your own kids to push them or put pressure on them. You don't even have to spend time with them or listen to them. My parents didn't push me. They parented me and taught me lessons of life, but they let me do things on my own and learn from my own mistakes. They would encourage me, but it wasn't like a life-or-death situation. Too many parents fall into that kind of head trip, and I think that is a big part of what is wrong with America.

It always amazes me when people hear about nightmare parents, like some of the parents on the professional tennis circuit, and somehow miss the fact that they are typical of how a lot of parents are all around the country. Tennis mothers are just one extreme example of the pushy, never-satisfied baby boomers who would rather pay for expensive lessons for their kid than sit down for a good heart-to-heart talk. They are just a painful reminder of how many parents out there somehow equate success as a parent with their child's success in some competitive endeavor that may or may not help prepare their child for life.

There is actually a lot of truth to the idea that behind every great tennis player, there is a psycho tennis parent, and I have played enough tennis to know. Sad to say, but you probably do need someone who pushes you very, very hard if you are going to make it at the top professional level, especially in an individual sport. But there's such a fine line. Too often the parents get overly involved. They want the media attention for themselves and the glory and the fame, too.

It's sad, because what you see are a lot of people who make it and make it big, but they have no relationship with their family once they make it because they realize their family is just completely nuts. That is a pretty standard pattern, actually. So often the parents are overly involved, to the point where it almost ruins them. And yes, there is no question that the same pattern translates into everyday life now, because there are so many parents out there who are pushing their kids to the extreme.

Look at stage moms, another wonderful breed. On VH1 the other day they were talking about mothers who are pushing their kids to go into acting so they can make it in the movies or at least appear in TV commercials. These parents are just crazy. They are living vicariously through their children and doing it so blatantly that it is unbelievable.

Two generations ago, a lot of parents were just exhausted from the Great Depression and World War II, and they took a more passive role as parents. That is pretty much what I hear from my parents and my grandparents. But as a result of that, the kids whom they raised grew up without any qualms about pushing their kids. They didn't see the dark side of it. So now it seems as if my generation is getting pushed like crazy to succeed. We are constantly given the message that the only way to feel good about yourself is if you show through your actions that you are better than everyone else. Everything has to be competitive.

I remember when I was growing up playing soccer and hearing a dad yelling and screaming at a seven-year-old kid because he was on the losing team. I mean, give me a break. Come on. What bothered that dad was just that the kid was on the losing side, and he just wore his son out verbally for that. I know a lot of kids who had to deal with that kind of thing and just didn't make it. They just shut down once they got older and could make their own choices.

The worst part of all is that the problem is only getting worse. I look at kids who are ten to fifteen years younger than me and just shake my head. Their parents are even more high-strung than the parents of my generation. It has gotten to the point where if you have a child, you might as well automatically proclaim the kid has attention deficit disorder. Parents are all so worried about whether their kids are normal, but they don't even know what normal is. So they decide their kids are crazy because they run around and have a lot of energy. Well, hello! Running around and having a lot of energy is *normal* for a kid. That's what they are supposed to do. But if you get after them all the time to sit down and be quiet, and if you discipline them for doing what any kid wants to do and what every kid has been doing forever, then you are really going to be messing that kid up.

Sure, kids need to learn that there are times when they need to sit down and be quiet and respectful. But if you want your kid to be like that all the time, then you are going to have real problems. Kids are going to be rambunctious, and, yes, sometimes they are going to be obnoxious. They are going to giggle and laugh about silly things and have fun playing games and being carefree. That's called being a kid, and it's something we all should get to do for a while before we turn into worried old parents. Anyone who expects their baby to pop out of the womb ready to start acting like a twenty-year-old had better think twice before having children.

Parents don't want to parent anymore. They would rather go to the doctor and get their kid on medication so the kid is sedated and won't bother the adults anymore. That is why so many kids are being told that they have ADD. Now parents almost want their kids to have ADD, because then when they take standardized tests, like the SAT or the ACT, they can take them without a time limit! How is that for a good deal, especially for parents who are obsessed that their kids are perfect and successful and go to a great school? I truly believe that is one reason why we see the ADD diagnosis abused so much.

But you know what? Somehow this world survived for millennia before we had ADD medicine. Somehow this country survived for more than two centuries. I don't know how it happened, but somehow we actually functioned as a nation. To hear people talk now, you would think that without medication for ADD and all these other ways to sedate children, we would be living in an unhinged, insane world. Doctors are going to go along with the charade. Sure, why not? Why should they turn down years and years of getting to charge that patient to come in for more visits and more prescriptions?

Parenting isn't always easy. I'm sure it can be tough sometimes when you have to discipline your kid and tell him to sit in the corner for a while, or if he's older, when you have to tell him he is grounded. But parents are given all these crutches to hide from the responsibilities of parenthood. Doctors are quick to give medication to drug kids into submission. Or parents head into the kid's school for a parent-teacher conference and turn the kid's story into a sociology lesson, when all the kid really needs is a swift kick in the rear end.

There's the whole debate now: Should you spank your children? I would be the first to admit that spanking kept me out of trouble. I was stubborn as a mule. I know y'all have a hard time believing that! But I was the kind of kid who literally knew when he was cruising for a bruising, as the old saying goes. I would wake up in the morning and just know I was going to get a whipping. I was 100 percent sure. I would put on an extra pair of underwear so it wouldn't hurt as much. Later on, maybe around the age of eleven or twelve, my parents started to change their tactics; they would ground me or take away my Nintendo.

I got into trouble for being disrespectful or lying, the normal things kids get in trouble for doing. But you know what? My parents spanked me, and it didn't scar me for life or anything like that. I don't have horrible memories. In fact, I don't remember it much at all, except one time my mother spanked me and I had to laugh at her because she couldn't even hit me hard enough for it to hurt. That's the only spanking memory I have.

One thing I think is really important is not being too quick to give a kid an out. When you say, "It's okay, little Timmy, you've got ADD," that gives him an out and sends the message that you don't expect him to succeed. I would say it's almost encouraging him to fail. It gives the kid an excuse for just about anything bad he might want to do.

Do I think I had ADD? Yeah, probably. I've had doctors say I could easily get on medication. But I think that would have been only a crutch. I made it. I learned discipline. I learned how to focus. To me it's horrible to get a kid on regular medication for ADD at a young age, because it opens him up to taking other stuff when he's older. Studies have shown that when you place a kid on medication when he's young, he's more susceptible to using other drugs later on.

Family values can help a child more than any drug. Family values tell you that good parenting does not have to be anything new or radical or cutting edge. Good parenting can be simple. It means disciplining your kids and helping your kids grow up to be whatever they are going to be. It doesn't mean you have to be a millionaire to be successful. You can be a good parent without your kid growing up to be a millionaire. Too many parents are so focused on turning their kids into big successes, they forget to teach them about right and wrong. They forget to teach them morality, or what it means to sell out, or when to say no, or how to say no. It's almost like: Do whatever you have to do, however you have to do it, because if you make it and are a success, then we will be proud of you.

A lot of parents are so consumed with their kids being perfect and being popular, and because they are living vicariously through them, they forget to teach them about just being themselves. Some people may be computer geeks and be completely happy with that. They don't have to be popular. But too many parents seem to decide almost before the kid is even born just how he should turn out. He should be skinny and good-looking. He should have blond hair and blue eyes. He should be popular and the captain of the football team. Everybody should think he's wonderful, and they should all want to be just like him. That way, our family looks great!

Do I really have to point out the obvious? Do I really have to say that not everyone is going to be the star quarterback? You have to take what life gives you and accept it and make the most of it. But parents put so much pressure on their children that a lot of kids end up failing because they know they have no chance of meeting the goals the parents put out there for them. I can remember teaching six-year-old kids tennis and having their parents come up to ask about them, and you could tell from the look in their eyes how distraught these parents were. They were worrying that one little kid was not hitting the ball as well as the next kid. You could tell these parents were tossing and turning at night, unable to sleep, because they were so worried that they might not have a tennis prodigy in the house.

"Should we give him lessons every day?" they would ask me.

I wanted to tell them to leave the kid alone. Maybe he would develop into a great athlete a couple of years later, or maybe not. But they were so concerned that their child be the best, they were ready to throw out massive amounts of money to try to make him better. It's so sad, because kids like that, even if they improve and get better, are never going to have any fun out on the tennis court. Their parents put so much pressure on them, the kids end up hating something they might have loved. That, I'm afraid, is the story of my generation, which has had to deal with far too many crazed parents who are too scared and too nervous just to sit back and let their kids be themselves. I hope we can at least learn something and not do such a number on our own kids.

PART IV

Heroes
and Anti-Heroes

CHAPTER 18

President "Rhymes with Witch"

It has been real entertaining watching Hillary Clinton set about defining a role for herself as a United States senator and would-be president. She made history by becoming the first former First Lady elected to the Senate, but the interesting part is not what she has done but how she has done it. Let's remember that not so long ago, especially early in Bill Clinton's presidency, hardly anyone liked Hillary. She spent so much time early in her husband's administration pushing controversial issues like health care and just getting slammed down left and right. People saw her as cold and power hungry and scheming.

Then her makeover began. How did it happen? Very simply. As soon as the Monica Lewinsky scandal hit with full force, Hillary was able to play the victim. She stood by her man. She was the faithful wife, willing to endure her husband's philandering, and suddenly people took a new look at her and liked what they saw. "Oh, what a strong woman," they all said. She was doing interviews all over the place, and she couldn't lose.

People wanted to like her. It wasn't always easy, because she has a real genius for rubbing some people the wrong way, but after the Lewinsky craziness, Hillary was a new woman.

That was the greatest thing that ever happened to her career. The funny part is, everyone always knew what was going on. There were always Bimbo Eruptions, and Bill really knew how to pick 'em, didn't he? Some who worked for Clinton would tell you over a beer that the man always has been a womanizer and always will be. They might tell you that Hillary was long past being mad at her husband for cheating, she was just mad that he was dumb enough to get caught. But so what? What mattered was that most people in the country felt they could relate to her all of a sudden as a long-suffering wife who had to live with a husband who was always disappointing her. She was given a free pass to play the victim, and she made the most of it.

That is how she has become so powerful. She gained a platform, and because there will always be an interest in anything she has to say, she's politically bulletproof now. It used to be that conservatives could attack her and score points right and left, she was such an easy target. But not anymore. Now you can't touch her. You can't beat up on so famous a victim. It just doesn't work. People won't stand for it. That would only backfire and make her even more popular, so she can do what she wants.

Would anyone ever have taken her seriously as a Senate candidate in New York, a state where she had never lived, if not for the Lewinsky saga? Heck no. But she knew what a strong hand she had to play, and she figured, why not? She saw an opportunity, and she jumped on it. It was kind of a joke at times. She took some criticism for wearing a Yankee cap at the White House in 1999, and she was so scared she hasn't worn a baseball cap again. She was not much of a speaker early in that race. But she hung in there and improved her political speeches, and a lot of voters warmed up to her.

People related to her because she was a strong, independent woman who had made it though controversy and had persevered. People find her intriguing, and that's understandable. It is just basic human nature. We all have troubles in our lives, but let's face it, not too many of us have had to deal with anything as awful as having a husband like Bill Clinton. Hillary gets brownie points because of that, and she can be very selective in what she chooses to make public and what she chooses to hide.

Living History was brilliant in that sense. Her book was not a huge success because people wanted to read up on her foreign-policy thinking or her position on China or on health care. And no one would rate Hillary Clinton among the best First Ladies in U.S. history. But everybody read her book to see what she would say about Monica Lewinsky and Bill Clinton. That's a good example of how she has it both ways. She would never have landed an $8 million advance on her book if she had not promised to talk about Monica, and she had no qualms about playing that card. She knows how valuable the Monica card is to her identity. She dealt with the topic in her book, she went out and sold the book, and the book jumped to the top of the best-seller lists and created all kinds of buzz. Everyone was talking about her again, and she loved it.

Men can't really attack her. To women, her story is empowering, because it shows that women can overcome even the worst adversity and still make it. So if a man attacks her, it's almost as if he is attacking all women or at least all women who have had some hardship in their lives. That shields her from any personal attacks, the fact that she has a reservoir of sympathy because of what she has been through—and everyone knows it. That is her most formidable political weapon, and she has used it skillfully, especially since the publication of *Living History* pushed her to another level of political stardom.

There's no question that she has become the most powerful figure in the Democratic Party and that, going into 2008, she has to be considered the favorite to get the nomination. She definitely wants to run for president. The amazing part is she was able to show enough patience and discipline to wait four more years. She has a good chance of emerging as the top Democratic candidate, and, to me, it will almost be like her running mate is Monica. Hillary learned a lot about power during her eight years in the White House, and no one wants to mess with her. People know that if you cross Hillary, she will do her best to mess you up. She can make or break your career as a Democrat, and that is why she will be so strong a candidate in 2008 if Bush wins reelection in 2004.

If she actually wins, that would be horrible. I'll say it right here in black and white: Hillary Clinton would be one of the worst presidents this country has ever seen. Maybe it would be different if we were going through a different period of our history and things were quieter around the world. But if anyone thinks we will have won the war on terror by 2008, they're crazy. The only way we will win that war is to keep fighting it year after year, and generation after generation, if need be. We need to be leaders in the world, and we need to make a strong case for our perspective, even when we are telling leaders of other countries things they do not want to hear.

A woman has every right to run for president, but let's face facts. I wouldn't support my own mother for president because the cold, hard reality is, leaders of other countries just will not have the same respect for a woman president of the United States that they would for a man who is president. If that sounds sexist, well, sorry, but I am just looking at the realities of doing business with other countries. There are leaders in many countries with which we are dealing now who would not even come to the table to talk to a woman president. That doesn't mean a woman isn't capable of doing a fine job as president. But we have to think about the image we project abroad, and leaders in many other countries would have no respect for a woman leader. They wouldn't negotiate and wouldn't communicate openly with a woman president. That would put our country in grave danger in foreign policy and undermine our position in every region of the world. Is that a sad commentary on other countries? Absolutely. Do we hope it will change with time? Of course we do.

But the truth is, women are low on the totem pole around the world, especially in third-world countries. The world just isn't ready for a woman U.S. president, even if we in the United States are, and having a woman as commander in chief would empower terrorists around the world. I don't think that's fair, but that's reality. I just don't see a woman commander in chief walking into a room at the United Nations and giving a speech and getting the kind of respect where people really shut up and listen. I just don't think they're going to take her seriously. That's what worries me in this. That's why I wouldn't have supported someone like Elizabeth Dole either.

If Hillary were ever elected president, I think she would change her colors so fast, our heads would be spinning. She has been careful to position herself as more of a moderate this last year or two because she knows that is the smart thing to do, and no one has ever doubted that Hillary Clinton is one smart lady. But if she got elected, she would go right back to her true character—100 percent liberal. She would not wait more than about five seconds before she would get back to pushing an extreme agenda that would alienate just about everyone in the country except perhaps in places like Berkeley, California, and New York, New York, and Cambridge, Massachusetts.

She would also have serious problems with her style. She's always been pretty short-tempered and thin-skinned. All that bunk about a vast right-wing conspiracy trying to undermine her husband? That would be just the beginning of what we would hear from her if she were president. She would probably make up a new conspiracy every week. People would get so tired of hearing her feel sorry for herself, they wouldn't listen to a darn word she said.

Hillary Clinton would just be miscast as president. She's all brimstone and fire. Her diplomatic skills are way below par. Do I think she'd make a great talk-show host? Absolutely! She could be the next Donahue. Sign her up! (But didn't he fail at that job? Oh yeah, he did.) Hillary is too brassy to be president. She's witchy, she's cranky, she's moody. People in New York like that. New Yorkers are blunt and quick to the point and don't like to be jerked around. But that stuff just doesn't fly across the rest of the country. I just think it would be complete gridlock in Washington if she were president. She would alienate so many people in the House and the Senate. She would have few allies. People either love Hillary Clinton or they hate her, and she's not very good at winning new friends over to her way of thinking.

People would also get really tired of being asked to pretend that the Clintons have a real marriage. We all know better, don't we? What they have is no marriage. An arranged marriage, maybe, or a marriage arrangement, but it's not a marriage in the sense that any decent person would use the word. I think their marriage is as dead as a doornail. I think it's a convenient marriage for political gain. You never see him with her. You just don't. They didn't even spend the last holidays together because she was gallivanting around the globe in Iraq and Afghanistan. What does that tell you?

But they will be side by side all the time when she is running for president. You can count on that. That is where family comes back into it. Hillary knows when to use families, and she knows that smart politics requires her to do that. She's going to have the dog out there, she and Bill are going to be holding hands, and she's going to have Chelsea out there, too. If she won, he would have to live in the White House, and they would have to pretend to be a real couple again. He's going to have to play his part. She stood by her man and saved his presidency. Now it will be his turn to return the favor and bite the bullet. What would they call him? The First Man? The First Husband? The real question I want to ask is: Would they let him have any interns?

I don't think we would have to worry very much about his having undue influence on her presidency, though. It is hard to imagine her sitting down and asking him, "Honey, what do you think I should do about this? How do you think I should handle this?" It will be a cold day in heck before that happens. She would rather become the second President Clinton to be impeached than give anyone the idea she's playing second fiddle to Bill again.

It would be something to watch him out on the campaign trail again. She won't be as dumb as Al Gore and leave the greatest living Democratic campaigner with nothing to do. Oh no. It will be like Bill is running for president all over again. He will be making almost as many campaign stops as her and doing just as many fund-raisers. He will be out there in the limelight right up until Election Day and then if she wins, that is when he will go back to doing his own thing.

What worries me is that this is a woman who knows how to get what she wants, and she has an open path to the presidency. If she plays her cards right and she doesn't have a sitting president to go up against, if Bush wins reelection, then she would have the Democratic nomination, and it would be an open seat in 2008. It's not going to be Dick Cheney she would be going up against. He's going to be too old, and his heart is in bad shape, so no way. It will have to be a fresh new Republican candidate, and if it's Bill Frist, well, he has not exactly been offering himself in a way that connects with the common man. He's a Vanderbilt type all the way.

If I was advising Hillary, I would tell her to beg and plead for Bill Frist to run for president against her. If he does, the way it is shaping up, I think she would win. The voters like a change from time to time, and after eight years of Bush, a lot of people will be ready for a change. People will be thinking: If it's not going to be Bush, let's try something completely different. Let's just get a little crazy and try having a woman president. That would be a different direction.

That is why Hillary is not running this year. She knows that a Republican era will have passed in 2008 if Bush wins reelection this year. In fact, she hopes and prays Bush wins, if she prays at all, that is. She doesn't want a Democrat to win. That's obvious! Where would that leave her? She would have to wait maybe another eight years. So that is why she won't work this year to get a Democrat elected and why her husband won't either. If John Kerry or John Edwards or some other Democrat were to beat Bush, that would be her worst nightmare.

Instead, she keeps working on her political makeover. If you had said in 2002 that Hillary Clinton would be criticizing President Bush for not sending enough troops to Iraq, everyone would have laughed at you. But that is just what she was doing in late 2003. She took a trip to Afghanistan and Iraq around Thanksgiving to boost her credentials as a presidential candidate. She wanted to be able to say, "I've been to Afghanistan, and I've been to Iraq. I would have sent more troops and fought this thing to the fullest." Well, it's easy to say that in hindsight, but the point is, I don't think that's what she believes. She is trying hard to change the public perception of her as a liberals' liberal.

She's going to become more of a champion for soccer moms, I'm sure. Education and family values are big for her, and she's going to be more in touch with conservative issues that are family-oriented. That is where you will see her continue to shift her positions and her political identity. She will become more involved with seniors and health care for seniors, because she will definitely want to court the older generation by scaring them with a lot of alarmist rhetoric. She will make herself seem more conservative, and more moderate, and it will all just be an act, an obvious political stunt. But the sad, scary truth is, it just might work. It just might get her elected, which would be a disaster for this country.

CHAPTER 19

Newt Gingrich,
Role Model—Not!

Newt Gingrich taught me most of what I know about politics, both good and bad. He taught me with his visionary leadership that there's nothing wrong with caring enough to think on your own and come up with fresh ideas about how to make this country better. His Contract with America and the Republican sweep of 1994 energized me and got me interested in politics when I was thirteen. I even have an autographed copy of his book *To Renew America.*

But Gingrich also taught me never to see politicians as more than messengers. They are not role models. They are not better people than the rest of us. If you put too much faith in them, they will disappoint you. If you look up to them, they will send you crashing to the ground. That was what happened to me when I found out that for all his skill on television, Gingrich was just a good marketing man who was living a life that totally went against what he was preaching.

Gingrich and Bill Clinton had one of the great political rivalries of our times, but it turns out they had a lot in common. They seemed like perfect foils for each other. Gingrich was supposed to be the anti-Clinton in all ways. He had a bold program and vowed that the Republicans would enact all of it within a year after winning a majority in the House for the first time in decades. Mostly, Gingrich fulfilled that promise during his time as Speaker of the House. But he also made a bid to present himself as a moral leader. He became a front man for the Republican Party and said that America needed to get back to family values.

We should have known better. If something seems too good to be true, it probably is. Even as he was working on his book about renewing moral values in America, Gingrich was having an affair with his much younger secretary. I shouldn't have been shocked by this, but I was. Here was a man I looked up to in many ways. I wanted to be like him when I grew up. But he turned out to be just a slick guy who found an angle to gain power, money, and, of course, sex. Everything from the Contract with America to his book about family values was just a load of junk to make him become more powerful.

Gingrich taught me a bitter lesson but a valuable one. He taught me to pay attention to how things really are, not how we hope they are or hope they will be. Liberals always want to see the world in terms of how it ought to be. They get lost in their dreams about what we could do if we could only change this and that and the other thing. Conservatives are more realistic and less sentimental. I happen to agree with a lot of the points that Gingrich made as Speaker of the House, and to this day his leadership has shaped who I am. But I've learned never to trust any politician to be anything more than very, very human, with all the human limitations and failings that come with that. I think that's a healthy perspective.

Political parties are overrated. I'm a Republican, but that doesn't mean I give up my right to think for myself. I don't mind saying that I've even voted for a Democrat. I voted for a strong Democrat candidate for mayor of Shelby County, Tennessee, over a so-called conservative Republican who spent so much of his own money trying to buy the election that he could have bought a small third-world country instead. The Democratic candidate was the better person for the job. He had experience and a reasonable plan to make the county a better place to live. The Republican just wanted to be called "Mayor" and get his name in the paper.

I'm glad Newt Gingrich opened my eyes to the reality that parties on both sides of the aisle have become mere puppets. Political parties are controlled by men and women who have no clue what the average American thinks because they are too busy kissing the rears of the rich and famous. We all know it, too. So the real question is: Whose fault is it that we have gotten to this point? That's an easy one: It's 100 percent *our own fault.*

We Americans have become too busy with our own lives. We have allowed the suck-ups to take control of our political parties because this is a nation so apathetic to politics. Our apathy has turned what used to be issues politics into big-business politics. Just look at the last several leaders of the Republican National Committee. These men have been completely out of touch with the average Republican, but we are the ones who let them hold the office. All they care about is making sure they make friends with a lot of rich businessmen and famous elected officials, so one day down the line they can run for office themselves. If they have the insiders' backing, they know getting elected will be a piece of cake.

It's enough to make you sick. We should all feel sick, and we should blame ourselves if we continue to do nothing. It's time for the average American to become more vocal and less passive. It's time we start to pay attention to what's going on, and I mean *really* pay some attention, not just listen to two minutes of news at the top of the hour. If we don't wake up and open our eyes, the things that make this country great will be gone forever, thanks to some little so-called smart guy in Washington whom we let get into a position of party leadership. I am tired of having people call my show and say, "I can't believe what's going on in Washington." Well, it's going on because we let it.

I will be the first to say that the Ronald Reagan days of the Republican Party are long gone. This party I used to love is far gone. That is why I don't toe the party line. Sure I am conservative, but I have talked to too many people in leadership roles who could care less about you and me so long as they keep getting reelected and keep getting their palms greased. Here's a little experiment I encourage all of you to try. The next time you disagree with something your party does, call your local congressman and see how much smoke he blows at you. Believe you me, many don't seem to care about you unless you have money, power, or fame.

We have to change the way the game is played. We need to get rid of the Washington rats and the rich kids, but this will happen only if the average voter gets involved. I don't want to make any false promises. It's not always exciting getting out there and trying to make a difference. The only way to make a dent is to be smart. We have to pick a person we think would do a good job and work to get him or her elected. That might be boring at times. It might be frustrating. But if we all do this, we can take back what was once ours.

Look back at the names and faces in American history books. Most of these men and woman didn't go into politics because they thought they were better than the average workingman. In fact, most elected officials didn't come from money. Most worked hard to prove themselves to others, and that is how they gained the trust of the communities that eventually elected them. The men who founded this country knew that if they failed, they would all be killed. What they did was totally for the good of their communities. The stakes were high then, and everyone knew who their elected representatives were. It's a sad fact that in today's America, most people can name the entire cast of *Friends* but cannot name their mayor, governor, congressman, or senator.

If you think about how much the government is involved in our lives, and how many hours we have to work just to pay our yearly taxes, it's amazing to me that we actually let second-rate, candidates win so many elections. We let these mediocrities run our lives because we are too busy to spend twenty or thirty minutes every other year to inform ourselves about who is running. Even when we are picking a new president, there are no guarantees that half the voting-age population will bother to show up and vote. Only 49 percent did in 1996. Just think about all that has happened since the last presidential election in 2000. We had September 11, the war in Afghanistan, the war in Iraq, and some economic ups and downs. I know at least one of these issues affected each of you directly. But still, I bet the turnout for this next presidential election coming up in November will be less than 50 percent again.

It's time to stop complaining and start getting involved. If we don't, my generation and the generation after mine won't be able to live the same lives my parents have. We are the only ones who can say that enough is enough. We are the only ones who can put good politicians back in office. The bottom line is, we have to invest our time and money in people we believe hold our views, no matter what side of the political spectrum they come from. The ugly reality for all of us to keep in mind is: We get the politicians we deserve. We will never have an abundance of great leaders until we the voters decide to go out and help a candidate whom we think is worthy. Most Americans polled say that when they hear the word *politician,* they think of a liar. If that's the case, why don't we do something about it?

Would you work for a company that lied to you all the time? Would you date or marry a person who lied to you nonstop? Would you overlook it if your kids lied to you regularly? I hope not. If you answered no to all these questions, then ask yourself: Why do we allow ourselves to give thousands of dollars a year to a government nobody trusts? Why don't we invest our time into making sure our interests are represented? Why don't we say okay, this year I'm going to help a candidate whom I think will be more than just another faceless, poll-driven hack?

We have lost the statesman mentality that helped lead this country for so long. Now we have a bunch of cut-off, clueless politicians running our lives, and that's because we the citizens are too busy or too scared to roll up our sleeves and get our hands dirty. I would love to see an average, normal American elected to the Senate. I would love to see an average woman elected as president of the Republican National Committee, or of the Democratic National Committee for that matter. We need real people in there, reminding the other politicians to cut out all the bull that is being sent to us every day. That goes for Republicans as well as Democrats.

A high-ranking Republican called me one day to tell me how angry he was that I was criticizing the party. "Remember, Ben, you don't cut off the hand of the person who feeds you," he told me. I thanked him for the advice, but I told him I was never going to become a Republican slave. I was never going to subject myself to the whims of the party and give up the ability to think for myself. We've become way too passive. We let the party leadership set the tone, which is to do whatever the party tells us to do, not listen to the voters back home, not fix the problems that the voters want fixed. All I can say is, the Republican Party better watch out for people my age. We're mad, and we're not going to be led by the nose.

Sending a message to all parties is a good place to start. You almost had to laugh looking at the left during the last presidential election. People supported Ralph Nader as a third-party candidate because they thought the Democrats and Republicans had become too similar. So Nader goes out and funnels off just enough votes to give George W. Bush the election. People criticized Nader voters for being shortsighted. But maybe everyone ought to follow their example. Maybe that's one way to shake things up a little. Maybe we should all vote for whichever candidate is best, whatever his or her party affiliation. When people walk into the voting booth and vote straight party line, they are doing a disservice not only to themselves but also to their beliefs, on top of hurting the country as a whole. It's time we stop complaining about how bad things are in this country and begin to find the best man or woman for the job. It's time we start to care about what a person has done and not done, before we write that person a check or give him or her our vote. It's time to start to care enough about our future that we take the time to find out what a candidate is all about.

My generation learned at a young age that no matter what people say, it does matter who we elect to high office. We all heard enough jokes about Bill Clinton's mischief to last a lifetime, but for people my age, the controversy over his fling with Monica Lewinsky came at an awkward time. It literally took away the innocence of a generation. Here we were, at an age when no one had talked to us before about oral sex, blow jobs, and thongs. Suddenly, these things were discussed all the time. You heard about them at the dinner table with your family. You heard about them everywhere. No one got tired of talking about these topics.

Young people are curious. Naturally, they are going to ask questions. "What is oral sex, Mom?" "What's a blow job, Dad?" "What's a thong?" Sex has changed completely for people my age. You took a whole generation and threw them into a world of sex, whether or not they were ready for that, and there is no way to undo that. I'm sure a lot of people had the same experience I did. I was thirteen or fourteen at the time. I had never talked about thongs. I had never looked to see if a girl had a panty line showing. I had never talked with anyone about blow jobs or oral sex.

Suddenly that whole world opened up. Everywhere you went, people were talking about Bill Clinton and Monica Lewinsky. Within five minutes, you could be having a very provocative conversation about sex. Bill Clinton could be your punch line. Especially for guys my age, that became very typical. You want to talk to girls about sex. You want to get into these sexy conversations. But it's always difficult. You feel awkward. You feel shy. Then suddenly you could make a little joke about Monica's thong or Monica's dress. It was too easy. You could open the door to the raciest discussion, all with a little joke straight from the headlines.

It was like, everybody does it. Heck, the president does it. Let's give it a shot! You weren't a pervert anymore if you brought it up. You weren't being offensive or gross. It became normal. My generation was blasted with the message that oral sex is no big deal. It has no consequences. You just look at how much everybody talks about oral sex on TV now, how much people talk about thongs. Or look at thong sales in general. They went through the roof after the story broke about Monica pulling up her skirt and showing Clinton her thong.

Once we've lost our innocence, there is no going back. I didn't know anyone who was having oral sex at thirteen or fourteen when I was that age. Now a lot of kids that age are having sex. Oral sex is rampant. You have companies marketing thongs to girls who are ten or eleven. Before it came out about Clinton and Lewinsky, if a mother had found a thong in a girl's drawer, the girl would have been grounded. Now, it's as if girls are uncool if they don't wear them. Some schools around the country didn't think it was even an issue last year if sixth-graders wore thongs to school. It's a peer-pressure thing. A girl says to her mom, "Everybody's wearing them. I don't want to get made fun of for having a panty line." There is no innocence anymore. There is no, "We kissed and made out." Now it's, "Did she go down on you? Did you get a blow job? Does she wear a thong?"

That's where I think people missed the point of how big an impact the Lewinsky story had on society. Sure, Clinton lied. Yes, he had an affair. But he also took away any respect or nervousness or fear that young people would normally have about sex. And when you take that away from an entire generation, that's a huge deal. Oral sex has become like making out used to be. There is no shame in it anymore. If you don't do it, you're not cool.

What we're talking about here goes far beyond just junior-high-school kids wearing thongs. Pop culture is always going to try to be provocative. That's the way to get people's attention. But now there's a kind of cult of outrageousness. The limits have to be tested constantly. You can draw a straight line from Clinton sex talk to the way Britney Spears and Christina Aguilera always push the limit. Even boy bands push the limit in the way they dance and the way they look. Clinton opened the door, and once it's open, everyone is walking through it. I think it even opened the door to reality TV shows and to sitcoms, where everybody sleeps with everybody else, and to music videos getting even raunchier. It opened the door to Britney Spears wearing a thong onstage at the music awards and nobody being shocked by that.

So where does that lead? The only way for Britney and Christina to shock anyone anymore is to have orgy-type videos or to kiss Madonna. That all goes back to Clinton and all the oral-sex jokes he inspired. A president should have our highest respect. He should offer an example to everyone, especially young people. So when you have him setting that kind of example, it makes it that much easier for everybody else to join in, because he's kind of the moral standard. Maybe that's not how it should be. We ought to find our own moral standards within ourselves. But a lot of people think of the president as a leader. You don't want your president to be somebody who is getting it from somebody half his age in the Oval Office of the White House.

There are lessons here for all of us to consider. We've let politics become a game. Until we stand up as individuals and demand better candidates, and better campaigns, we're going to find ourselves stuck with officeholders who are a national embarrassment. Just look at Newt Gingrich and Bill Clinton. Here they were, political opposites by all appearances. But they were actually being advised by the same man. A political consultant named Dick Morris was a close adviser to both. He would literally meet with Gingrich in the morning and head over to the White House to meet with Clinton in the afternoon. Forget that it was a conflict of interest. How could a man be advising politicians who are polar opposites unless he has absolutely no convictions himself? He was just selling out to the highest bidder. And look how it all worked out. Gingrich turned out to be a hypocrite, lecturing us about values when he was having an affair with his secretary. Clinton cost a generation its innocence with his reckless sexual behavior. And Morris, their adviser, ended up getting arrested for seeking out the services of a prostitute. To all of them, politics was just a game. Until we demand more from our leaders, we'll all be the ones who lose.

CHAPTER 20

My Favorite American

My whole life I've had the feeling that a little luck was on my side. I think it goes back to my birth. If I'd been born eight months earlier, I'd have been a Jimmy Carter baby, and I'd really have hated that. Instead, I was born on August 28, 1981, seven months and eight days after Ronald Reagan was sworn in as president. I don't remember a lot from his eight years in office, since I was so young, but they always say our attitudes and assumptions are shaped in our first few years. I've never had any doubt that I gained a sense of optimism and patriotism in those years that I don't ever expect to lose. Reagan set an upbeat tone and gave us all the message that we never had to apologize for loving our country or believing in its greatness. I'm so grateful for having that message deeply engrained in my consciousness, I'll always see Ronald Reagan as my favorite American.

I have only one clear memory of the Reagan presidency. That was January 20, 1989, the day he and Nancy left the White House and climbed aboard the helicopter, Marine One, for the trip back to California. I'll never forget the way Reagan looked that day in his white scarf and overcoat, red-cheeked and fit-looking, even at age seventy-seven, as he waved good-bye with grace and dignity and gave us one last it's-going-to-be-all-right Reagan grin. It was amazing. He had to be churning inside with so much bittersweet emotion, but he was joking and telling so many stories that day that Nancy had to ask him to be quiet. "Ronnie, let's just enjoy these moments," she told him. But Reagan was determined to stand tall and, most important, be himself. He wanted to enjoy every minute at center stage, where he always felt comfortable. I think that day tells us a lot about who Ronald Reagan was as a man and how his first instinct was always to connect with people using basic, homespun common sense.

"They called it the Reagan Revolution. Well, I'll accept that, but for me it always seemed more like the great rediscovery, a rediscovery of our values and our common sense," Reagan said that day in his last speech from the White House. "Common sense also told us that to preserve the peace, we'd have to become strong again after years of weakness and confusion. So we rebuilt our defenses, and this New Year we toasted the new peacefulness around the globe. . . . Once you begin a great movement, there's no telling where it will end. We meant to change a nation, and instead, we changed a world. Countries across the globe are turning to free markets and free speech and turning away from the ideologies of the past. For them, the great rediscovery of the 1980s has been that, lo and behold, the moral way of government is the practical way of government: Democracy, the profoundly good, is also the profoundly productive."

Reagan offered a warning that day about how important it was to teach the young about who we are as Americans and what that means. He worried that was being lost. He remembered how when he was young, patriotism went without saying. "We absorbed, almost in the air, a love of country and an appreciation of its institutions," he said. "If you didn't get these things from your family you got them from the neighborhood, from the father down the street who fought in Korea or the family who lost someone at Anzio. Or you could get a sense of patriotism from school. And if all else failed you could get a sense of patriotism from the popular culture. The movies celebrated democratic values and implicitly reinforced the idea that America was special. TV was like that, too, through the mid-sixties."

If Reagan was giving that speech today, he would still be worried about popular culture, especially television, but to me it's amazing to think about how much my own experience was like what he talked about. Growing up, I absorbed a love of country and an appreciation of all our blessings. A lot of that came from my parents, sure, but it went beyond their influence. Reagan's eight years in office left people feeling better about themselves and their lives. He left them feeling better about our history and our future, and it was just like he said, that love of country was in the air when I was growing up. He made it honorable and respectable to be proud of the red, white, and blue. I still am, and no one can ever take that away from me.

Another of my earliest memories was watching all of those people standing on top of the Berlin Wall on November 9, 1989. I'll admit, it was a little confusing for me, watching that on television. I lived in a free country. I couldn't imagine that leaders in other countries built long barriers with barbed wire on top to keep their people caged up like animals. But even just watching on TV, that was a thrilling day. The people who were ripping loose chunks of the wall looked so happy, so relieved, so human. Even the CNN anchors were kind of shocked; it was so hard to believe that the people of East Berlin were really free to leave.

There were parties that night on the same ground where many people had been shot trying to escape communism. People were walking over the dirt of no-man's-land, where spotlights used to roam, looking for any sign of movement to tell the snipers where to shoot. People spent months tunneling under that same ground, they wanted freedom so much; others built balloons to float to safety. One family I heard about spent more than a year building a large balloon, careful to keep it a secret from the government and even from their neighbors, who might have turned them in to the Stasi. When the family finally had their balloon ready, and had loaded everyone up to try to escape, the winds were wrong. To their horror, they found out when they landed that they were still in East Germany, the so-called Germany Democratic Republic. So what did they do? They went back to work and built another balloon and tried again. And found their way to freedom.

The fall of the wall was such a great day for freedom, and it would never have happened if it wasn't for Ronald Reagan's leadership. Liberals didn't want to admit it at the time, but history will offer a clear verdict. Reagan's leadership brought down that wall, and it brought down the whole Soviet Union. He had the guts to call it an "evil empire," and he was right. He framed the issue that way because he always tried to see problems the way real people did and not get caught up in all that professional politician stuff. That was how it was when he visited Berlin in June 1987 and gave a speech near the Brandenburg Gate. His advisers were against pushing Mikhail Gorbachev too hard. But Reagan had no stomach for caution. Some things just have to be said, loud and clear, for the whole world to hear, and so Reagan came right out and laid it on the line.

"In the 1950s, Khrushchev predicted: 'We will bury you,'" Reagan said that day with the Brandenburg Gate behind him. "But in the West today, we see a free world that has achieved a level of prosperity and well-being unprecedented in all human history. In the Communist world, we see failure, technological backwardness, declining standards of health, even wants of the most basic kind—food. Even today, the Soviet Union still cannot feed itself. After these four decades, then, there stands before the entire world one great and inescapable conclusion: Freedom leads to prosperity. Freedom replaces the ancient hatreds among the nations with peace. Freedom is the victor. . . .

"General Secretary Gorbachev, if you seek peace, if you seek prosperity for the Soviet Union and Eastern Europe, if you seek liberalization: Come here to this gate! Mr. Gorbachev, open this gate! Mr. Gorbachev, tear down this wall!"

Wow. Even now, those words have so much power, it's almost like hearing a gunshot that echoes to every corner of the globe. No one could believe it at first. American liberals couldn't handle it. European leftists thought Reagan was being hopelessly naive. Even Reagan's own staff was horrified. Not too many people know this, but that speech came very close to being censored. Reagan's own advisers didn't want him to give it.

It's an amazing story. This guy named Peter Robinson was a young White House speechwriter at that time, and he was sent ahead to West Berlin to hang out for a while and kind of get the mood of the people. He was at a dinner party when a well-off Frenchwoman told him, "Well, if your president is coming, tell him to tell Gorbachev to tear down the wall." Robinson smiled at his good luck. He knew he was going to write a speech that would be remembered long after he was gone. "Reagan will like that," he told the Frenchwoman. He wrote up the speech, and he knew he had something special. But he had a problem. He was sure Reagan's handlers would not want him to deliver anything that provocative. So what did he do? He went straight to the president and handed him a copy of the speech, and, of course, Reagan loved it. But his staff hated it. No, no, no, they all screamed. You can't give this speech! The State Department told him no. The Defense Department said no. Even the CIA told him no. They all made sure that another speech, something nice and bland, was prepared for Reagan to give instead. They asked him to promise he wouldn't include the "tear down this wall!" line.

I think that might have been the most important moment in Reagan's presidency. He was literally in the limousine on his way to the Brandenburg Gate to give his speech, and he was still mulling over what to do. This was a president who trusted his advisers. He went against their advice only if he really felt strongly. And on this he felt strongly. He turned to his aide Ken Duberstein, next to him in the limo, and said, "All the boys at State are going to kill me, but I've got to use that line. I've got to tell him to tear down that wall."

So he did. And it's a good thing, too. I remember watching with my parents the night the wall came down, and I remember talking with them about what a great day that was for freedom. My parents were really excited about all the incredible changes taking place in the world at that time, none more spectacular than the Berlin Wall tumbling, and my grandparents were excited, too. In fact, they have friends in Europe who went to Berlin to see for themselves how different the city looked with the guard towers emptied and the wall breached. They sent me a piece of the Berlin Wall, and I still have it. It's one of my most prized possessions. Sometimes I pick it up and try to imagine it when it was still part of the wall, blocking people from freedom. I keep that piece of the wall to remind me that we can never take freedom for granted.

Reagan changed the world because he knew who he was and always trusted his common sense. That's why Reagan is the one politician alive during my lifetime whom I would have most liked to have met. Heck, I'd have liked to sit down for a long talk with Reagan. It's not so much that I'd have wanted to ask him about anything in particular, although, of course, it would be priceless to hear him tell a few jokes or a few stories about his days in Hollywood or about sitting down to the negotiating table with Gorbachev. Mostly, I'd have liked to get an up-close look at Reagan being Reagan.

I think of myself as someone with his feet firmly on the ground, and that was how Reagan was. He was a common man all the way. He wasn't a Harvard graduate. He didn't come from money. He didn't inherit politics like the Kennedys did. He was kind of a P. T. Barnum of his own career. He just made it happen, and he was never afraid to be himself. It didn't bother him if people laughed at him. He liked to laugh at himself, too. How many politicians would have the good sense to relax with a favorite movie before a summit? That was what Reagan did. He watched *The Sound of Music.* He knew that his major asset was always his personality and his good sense, not his knowledge of throw weights or ICBMs and SLBMs. He didn't feel any particular need to try to be something he wasn't. Being himself had worked before, and he expected it would work again. That was why he never seemed like a career politician, because he didn't see himself that way.

You learn a lot about someone from his sense of humor. Reagan always liked a good joke, and his jokes were his way of knowing where he stood. A lot of the campus radicals hated him back in the 1960s when he was governor of California. That was especially true in Berkeley, where Reagan sent in National Guard troops after some trouble broke out over a patch of university-owned land the hippies decided was a People's Park. The radicals in Berkeley didn't like Reagan, and he didn't like them, either. He built his campaign for governor around his vow to clean up "the mess" in Berkeley, and he later told people: "I had a nightmare about going broke. I dreamed I owned a Laundromat in Berkeley." During one of his debates with Walter Mondale in 1984, he put an end to talk that he was too old at seventy-three by cracking: "I will not make age an issue of this campaign. I am not going to exploit for political purposes my opponent's youth and inexperience." And most famously, on May 30, 1981, even with blood coming out of his mouth after being shot by John Hinckley, he turned to Nancy and told her, "Honey, I forgot to duck," which was what Jack Dempsey had said to his wife after losing a 1926 fight to Gene Tunney. Reagan told doctors at the hospital that day: "I just hope you're Republicans."

Some people never warmed up to Reagan, but even a lot of people who were opposed to his ideas came to respect and like him. That was pretty incredible, especially in California, which has always been known as a more liberal state. To launch his political career there, where a lot of people didn't agree with his politics but believed in the man anyway, that says a lot about his character. He was one of those rare people who inspire a basic trust. People felt that he believed deeply what he was saying, so they weren't as skeptical of the details as they would be with most other people in public life. That's the mark of a true leader, someone who can be a leader not only of like-minded people but of all people, whatever their beliefs.

Reagan did not mind if you disagreed with him. In fact, he liked it. He took his ideas seriously and was glad when he inspired strong reactions in others, both positive and negative. The important thing was to be thinking about the big issues and knowing where you stood. Enemies were good. If you had enemies, it meant you were showing leadership. Your enemies helped define you. The Berkeley radicals, the tax-and-spend liberals, the blame-America-first crowd—all were useful foils for Reagan. They were not just people who happened to see things differently than he did, they were bitter enemies to be railed against at every opportunity. That was the way to win a fight, Reagan knew, to keep in mind who you were fighting against and to keep pushing the fight aggressively and relentlessly, even when it didn't look as if you had any chance of carrying the day.

Reagan understood strength. He changed my views on the military. Seeing how he beefed up the military more than any other president, and mostly never fired a shot, showed me that intimidation works. It's true. Usually the kids at school who were bullies were the big guys, so you didn't mess with them. It works that way with countries, too, and Reagan knew it. He'll be remembered as someone who thought beyond the World War II era and ahead to a new era and a new kind of thinking, which was to keep yourself safe and take care of yourself. I think George W. Bush is trying to emulate Reagan in terms of the way he does things. It's that same lesson about intimidation and about how it pays to be the bully. That way you can kind of take the attitude of, "Look, I don't want to have to use it, but I have a big, powerful military here that I'll use if I have to." We can all follow Reagan's example and never be afraid to be ourselves and to stand up for our beliefs, no matter how much opposition they might inspire. It worked for Reagan, and it's worked for me so far.

CHAPTER 21

What Republicans Can Learn from Bill Clinton

L
ike most conservatives, I celebrated January 20, 2001, as a national holiday. That was the day Bill Clinton packed up his boxes and left the White House forever. Yee-hah! I was overjoyed. Slick Willie had finally become a *former* president. His time had come to work the lecture circuit shamelessly and to try to stay out of Hillary's way. He'd been shrunk down to size, and we could safely ignore him, right? Actually, no. Clinton failed in many ways, but he was a master politician. You could even call him a political genius. He was smart enough to borrow heavily from Ronald Reagan, and future Republicans ought to be smart enough to learn a thing or two from how Clinton went about being president.

I know, I know. Any praise for Clinton makes a lot of you want to barf. But a wise man once told me you should study your enemies and learn from their strong points. He also told me they wouldn't be your enemies if they didn't have strong points. Given all of Clinton's legendary weaknesses, it goes without saying that he had his strengths. Otherwise he'd never have survived a single day, let alone become the first Democrat since FDR to serve two full terms.

What was Clinton's secret? Simple. He was smart. We're not talking school smarts here. Forget that stuff. Clinton was people smart. He always knew what made people tick. He had a knack for sensing what was important to them. That is why Clinton was so good at working a room. He connected with people in a way they remembered later. Even to this day, Clinton can energize a crowd. When he talks, everyone listens. When he smiles at people, they smile back.

The last thing the Republican Party can afford is complacency. Look what happened to Newt Gingrich and his followers when they got complacent. Winning one election is never enough. You always have to be thinking two, three, four elections ahead. Unfortunately, far too many of the individuals in leadership positions in the Republican Party are so stuck on themselves, they think they have it all figured out. They think they have all the answers. They could never in a million years show enough humility to understand that it makes sense to learn from others. That's just plain foolish. That's a recipe for frittering away your gains. That's a surefire way to wake up one day and realize you have absolutely no clue about the average, everyday American and what his concerns and priorities are.

Bill Clinton always understood the importance of connecting with average Americans. He never wanted to give the impression, even for a minute, of caring only about the wealthy and special interests. Sure, he sucked up to interest groups and, in reality, cared more about them than about the average citizen. But you would have never known that from watching him on TV.

Everyone always talked about what a policy wonk Clinton was, and he loved to dig into the details of a policy. But from the early days of his campaign for the White House, he understood that detailed position papers are never enough. The first President Bush left himself vulnerable with his "Read my lips, no new taxes" pledge. That was an easy target, and Clinton took advantage of that vulnerability. But he was smart enough to go beyond the blame game. He wasn't just concerned about reading the right line from a cue card. He wanted to talk to real voters and form his own ideas about what they cared about, whether or not he planned to do anything about it.

Clinton reinvented politics with the concern he showed for voters. It became a joke, Clinton's "I feel your pain" reputation. But it was a joke based on a genuine phenomenon. The man convinced people he cared. They really had the feeling he was different from the others and was genuinely concerned about them. What politician—from either party—would not love to have the same political asset?

Political campaigns are usually built on negativity. I'd say that 99.9 percent of the people who run for office rely on point-the-finger campaigns. All they do is tell you what the other person did wrong or didn't do. That's what the high-priced political consultants tell them to do. So they fill the airwaves with negative ads and make vague promises about doing a better job than whoever it is they are trying to replace. That wasn't how Clinton operated.

Republicans spend way too much time talking about what the Democrats haven't done. A lot of the points are good, but when you repeat them over and over, and never talk about anything else, it just gets annoying. It makes it look as if you have no idea of what you want to do to help the average American. It makes you look like a whiner who doesn't have enough backbone to stand up for his own ideas and instead has to spend all his time attacking someone else.

This was true even after the amazing success of the Contract with America, a great moment for all conservatives. For the first time in my life the Republicans showed a truly united front. They got organized and stayed organized. They had a plan. They had a time frame for action. They put it all together and got people to the polls, and, before you knew it, the Republican Party gained control of the House again for the first time in more than four decades.

But the Republicans' unity fell apart. Egos bounced off egos. Too many Republican leaders wanted to control the party's agenda so they could take credit for the good things that were happening. They started sniping at one another. They beat one another up. The party soon found itself divided, and by the next election we gave back to the Democrats almost everything we had gained. You have to maintain a united front and make sure that you really care about ideas and helping people. This is what Clinton did so well.

However else history judges Clinton, we can all agree that he was a fighter. Sometimes he made foolish choices. Why he let gays in the military become an issue during his first days in the White House will probably always be a mystery. But he had a stubborn streak, and often, if he decided he was going to get something done, he would keep working toward that goal long after many others would have given up.

He wanted gun-control legislation, even if it took all eight years of his presidency. He simply refused to let the issue go away, despite the huge influence of the National Rifle Association. His strategy was simple, but inspired. He literally forced the Republicans to pass the Brady Bill by proving to them, again and again, that he was going to seize on every chance he had to make them look bad for not taking action on it. Every single time there was a shooting, he pounced. He cited it as fresh evidence of how much we needed the Brady Bill. He used every school shooting to push for the bill. Was it rank opportunism? Did Clinton use kids' dying to gain a tactical advantage? Sure he did. And it worked. He was relentless and imaginative in using every resource at his disposal to keep the Brady Bill in the public mind. He drove the Republicans crazy with his relentlessness. They finally had to throw up their hands and say, "Okay, you can have your bill."

Clinton did what it took to get things done. Given all the hot air and entrenched interest groups in Washington, that's what he had to do to make any kind of difference. He had to force the issue. Unfortunately, the Republican Party does this about as well as I would do playing Tiger

Woods in a round of golf. We need to learn how to be fighters. I don't mean just here and there, firing up our outrage for a good sound bite. I am talking about sticking with an issue for the long haul, no matter what the other side does. The Democrats know that we aren't good fighters. They smell our weakness. That's why they continue to control so much of what goes on in Washington. They have used the art of badgering very well. Even after they lost control of the House and the Senate, they have still been able to block Republican ideas.

The Americans want their leaders to be fighters. That's a big part of our national identity. Reagan understood this so well. He really believed in the idea of a leader, even an American president, riding tall in the saddle. Overeducated eggheads on campus and in Washington laughed that off as naive, but to regular people, it made sense. Clinton and Reagan both hated to lose. They *really* hated to lose. Too many in the current Republican leadership see it all just as a job or a spectacle. They don't play for keeps. They need to learn from Clinton that losing is losing, no matter what the issue is. They need to learn that the people who voted them into office have a right to expect them to stick up for their principles. We didn't send you there to wear expensive suits and get expensive haircuts or expensive hairpieces and worry all the time about being politically correct. We sent you there to work for something. Maybe you didn't get the memo, but the Democrats have been making fools out of you. So Mr. Republican Leader, if you don't think you are cut out for this job, then please go take some fluff job in the corporate world and leave the real work to someone who has a little passion.

Too many Republicans have looked at Clinton's political skills as some kind of random, freakish talent. That's a cop-out. Clinton worked for his successes. He had great political instincts most of the time. He felt as if he understood the way real people would respond, and often he was right. But this wasn't some trick he pulled. He put a lot of thought and a lot of work into reaching out to people on a level most politicians don't understand. He tried hard to connect with them in at least some areas of their personal lives. He gave people the sense that for all the eloquence, for all the trappings of office, he was a lot like them in the basic ways that matter.

I call this the McDonald's Method. It was brilliant. Too many politicians are out of touch with regular people. They run for president and don't even know what it's like to shop for their own groceries. But what's more deeply American than loving fast food? And what president has shown one-half—heck, one-tenth—as much enthusiasm for fast food as Bill Clinton? I think that when anyone thinks of Bill Clinton now, the second image that comes to mind (right, the second) is of Clinton chowing down on a tray full of fast food. But when it came to fast food, Clinton paid for his appetite by showing some discipline. Think of all those mornings he was out there jogging. Think of how sad he often looked, huffing along in the hope of losing a pound or two so he could load up again on pizza or burgers or hot dogs.

Most Americans can't get enough fast food. But most Americans also feel they are too fat and need to lose weight. So here you had Bill Clinton constantly dealing with these same issues in his own life and doing it right there on national television for all of us to see. Clinton could have been too embarrassed to let people see him wrestling with the fast-food urge and sweating through all those morning jogs to make amends. But he was open about it. That showed America that he was a real person. It was a lot like Oprah. What's the first thing that comes to mind when you think of Oprah Winfrey? Weight loss, of course. That was the main issue she used to connect with a large audience. Hey, it worked. And she used it to trickle down into every imaginable area of self-help. She even gave us Dr. Phil.

Clinton would go jogging almost every morning when he was running for president, and the cameras would be there right behind him. This is a healthy thing to do, and many Americans would love to say they did the same thing every day. It made people feel good to see a leader taking care of himself by running. It also showed discipline. On the other hand, Clinton also knew people love to eat junk food. So where did he run? He ran straight to the nearest McDonald's. Then when he got there he would eat some unhealthy meal and sit around talking to the locals. All he had done was run and eat, but he had the eyes and ears of a nation.

People laughed, sure they laughed. But when they were laughing at Clinton for his funny-looking jogging, and his fast-food meals, they were laughing the way you laugh at your neighbor Bob or your uncle David or your aunt Sue. People were entertained, and they got used to thinking of Clinton as one of them. This was an invaluable political asset. Clinton felt it and used it. He showed up at the local hangout, and he talked to real people about what was on their minds. They talked back. They shared their thoughts with him, because he seemed like one of them.

Clinton heard the coffee talk of the nation, and he had his finger on the pulse of the average man in a way few politicians ever have. He heard what they had to say about how to change government's role in their lives. That wasn't the only way he got information, of course. He was paying some polling company to collect data, too. But he was also getting information himself. Polling, my friends, does not win elections. What wins elections is having the kind of real, personal interaction with people that stays with you and makes you alert to any shifts in public opinion. A poll does not talk, but people do.

Clinton sometimes knew what people thought before they did themselves, and that was because the man really did listen. He had his own way of working a room. He didn't just walk around shaking as many hands as possible. He would sit down with you and have a cup of coffee. He would ask about your background. He would ask about your family life. He would ask about your problems. He would ask about most anything that happened to come up and then sit there listening, really listening, as you gave him your answer. I can't name a single Republican candidate who has done this during my lifetime.

Republicans are masters of coming into a room, shaking every hand that gets waved in the air, and grinning and saying good-bye and getting the heck out of there, all while still being on schedule. Sure, a lot of people get to meet you that way. But what did you take away from that room? Did you gain any real information about what people are worried about? Or what they want to change? Or even what they like about your campaign? No way. All you did was make an appearance and take some pictures and get back into your limo thinking you just picked up a bunch of votes. This may have worked in the past, but it won't work in 2004.

Clinton was always falling behind schedule. This drove people crazy, and they were always complaining about it. But he knew what he was doing. If he's there talking to someone making minimum wage about his problems, his hopes, and his dreams, even as his staff members are saying, "Mr. President, we really have to be moving along," and he's just waving off his staff, nodding his head in that way of his and listening some more, that really makes an impression. It forms a connection. Compare that to Republicans who will pose for a picture only if you're a fat-cat donor who can fork over $5,000 or more to the campaign. I'm not saying Clinton didn't suck up to political contributors. Of course he did. But he made time for the little man, too. Republicans need to learn from that example. They need to reconnect with the average man. The party leadership has no clue what the average American is thinking. All they know is what the latest poll tells them.

Think about this for a second. Clinton faced more political disasters than any president since Nixon. Yet even after Whitewater and Gennifer Flowers and Bimbo Eruptions and the whole mess leading up to his impeachment, he still won reelection and stayed in office. How amazing is that? Even after he looked into the camera and lied to every American about having the affair with Monica Lewinsky, his job performance ratings were still incredibly high. How damning is that for the Republican Party? Americans thought that even after all he had done wrong, he was better for the job than any Republican in the entire United States. That tells you that the American people didn't feel that the Republican Party had any clue as to what their needs were.

The Republicans were so excited about finally getting Clinton, they lost sight of how regular people were thinking. No one likes a liar. The people were disgusted with Clinton at times. But the bottom line was, the regular people out there still had bigger problems than thinking about Clinton's affair. They were worried about school shootings. They were worried about Social Security going bankrupt. They were worried about a lot more than what the obsession of the week was in Washington, D.C. This is where the Republicans continue to drop the ball in election after election. They point out everything the Democrats are doing wrong, but they forget that this does nothing to make the seniors down at the coffee shop feel better about getting their Social Security checks. This does nothing to make the mother of two feel safer about sending her kids to a substandard school.

When Clinton hit rock bottom, he didn't wait for some poll to tell him what to do. Clinton did what got him to where he was. He got out there again. He went out and talked to the people not at the top of the totem pole but at the bottom. All the while the Republicans were doing everything they could to nail the man to the wall in hearings, in investigations, and on the Sunday-morning news shows. But Clinton proved he could do almost anything he wanted, short of killing someone, as long as the voters felt he was connecting with them and listening to their concerns. If he did that, they would vote for him again and again.

I believe in the platform of the Republican Party, most of it anyway. Unfortunately, the platform will never have a real chance until the leaders of the party get their heads out of the sand and start to listen to the common man's concerns. It's pathetic that the Republicans lost a presidential election to a soon-to-be-impeached president. Republicans need to learn that if you want to get elected, you have to run candidates who can connect with people. I am sorry, but it's going to be hard for a minimum-wage worker to get excited about yet another Republican CEO running for president. Why should they? The two have nothing in common. One is a multimillionaire, and the other is living paycheck to paycheck. And the millionaire never seems to have time to sit down with the man in the coffee shop during his campaign swing because he might be late to the next $500-a-plate lunch across town.

Personality matters. I mean *real* personality, not something that is faked. Bob Dole is a funny guy. Anyone who saw him in the Senate over the years before he ran against Bill Clinton for president could tell you that. Dole had a snappy wit. He could be sarcastic, and also very funny. But none of that came out when he was running against Clinton. Dole tried to act presidential in some buttoned-down and repressed kind of way, instead of just acting natural.

It was almost sad to see the contrast later on. Once the election was behind him, he was himself again. He was funny. He did a great ad for Pepsi with Britney Spears. Who can forget the "down boy" line from the commercial, referring to the fact that he takes Viagra? Heck, he even did Viagra commercials. He went back to being a funny old guy. I remember watching him on *The Late Show with David Letterman* and yelling at the TV, *"Why didn't you act like that during the elections?"* Dole had the whole audience eating out of his hand. Letterman would have voted for him after that appearance.

If Dole had acted normal instead of listening to some young Republican consultant who told him to act presidential, he would have won that election. Dole lost because he looked old and out of touch, even more out of touch than the Republican Party as a whole was that year. Talk about a wake-up call. So please, if you're running for any office on the Republican ticket, *please* be yourself and stop trying to act like an elected official. Remember, Americans in general don't like politicians, so why would you want to look or act like one.

If I were grooming a person to run for president, the first thing I would tell him is, learn how to play the drums. Think about how cool it would be for an older guy to play the drums onstage with some awesome band during an election year. I am telling you, that would pick up more votes than any speech you could ever give. Look at how it worked for

Clinton. I really do believe that what put him over the top during his first election was the fact that he played the sax on MTV and on Arsenio Hall's show. There is no way a Republican would have done that. If you can play something, then do it. Clinton was living out every man's dream to be a rock star for a day, and that connected with people. The Republican Party needs to stop taking themselves so seriously and start making sure they are finding a way to connect with normal everyday Americans.

CHAPTER 22

Donald Rumsfeld, a Hero for Our Times

You know what I really hate about liberals? They're so sneaky. They wait and wait and wait until they think someone is vulnerable. They don't have the guts to go after a strong leader directly, so they just back away until they sense an opening and then make their move. A perfect example of that is Donald Rumsfeld. During the Iraq war, he was everyone's hero. He was a true leader. A man with the courage of his convictions. A master of the press briefing. Then a little time goes by, and things aren't so easy in Iraq, and now suddenly Rumsfeld is everyone's favorite villain. Well, you know that? To me that just shows what a true hero he is.

Heroes are chosen by events. They are made by how they respond to history. Rumsfeld was the ideal leader for this country in the days and weeks and months after September 11. That was such a crazy time. Everything about how we saw the world and our place in the world had been suddenly, violently changed. We were all in shock. We were all stunned and confused. Even President Bush seemed uncertain and confused that first day, when Air Force One was rerouted away from Washington and Karl Rove told reporters it was because of a threat called directly into the White House. Later, Rove admitted that wasn't true. The president showed he was a leader in the days after that, especially when he visited Ground Zero. But in those first few hours, no one was as quick to rise to the occasion as Donald Rumsfeld.

Sometimes a little cockiness is a good thing. Sometimes a little arrogance comes in handy. Those qualities gave Rumsfeld a clear sense of purpose. He wasn't interested in second-guessing himself or in getting slowed down by too many distractions. No, he knew it was time to step up and show strength and resolve. He had a firm plan. He had a clear sense of mission. No one who listened to Rumsfeld had any doubts that this was a man with a clear vision of the direction we had to take after September 11.

People slept better at night knowing that someone as intense and charismatic as Donald Rumsfeld was clearly in charge. Let's not forget, those were scary times. People expected another terrorist attack. They expected more bombings. Airports became danger zones where security was so intense, flying became a nightmare. The anthrax scare led to wave after wave of panic over the threat of bioterrorism. That sense we had always had that we were protected by bodies of water on each side of us suddenly vanished. We didn't feel protected at all anymore. We felt unsafe and vulnerable.

Donald Rumsfeld understood that. He soothed our worries and calmed our fears. "Look, I'm taking care of you," he told us. "I understand these people. I know what's going on." He let the world know he was going to adopt a take-no-prisoners approach to fighting terrorism. He took a no-BS approach, and I think that's why Americans embraced him. Was he a little fanatical? Sure, of course, he was. But that's what we needed from our defense secretary at the time. He wanted a clear break with previous attempts to deal with terrorism, and he understood that September 11 gave him a way to push his more radical ideas.

His message was, "Look, we're not going to sit down at the table and negotiate. We're not going to have peace talks with you. We're not going to play the diplomatic game. We're going to come after you, and we're going to finish you off." He was a tough guy, but he was our tough guy, and that felt good. He was saying, "I don't negotiate. I stand behind what I say. I'm going to do what I say, and I'm not going to mess around with anybody who's trying to stall me. I want more funding. I want more troops. And I want them now."

He brought style to his role, too. I remember a movie that came out about ten years ago called *City Slickers,* with Billy Crystal and Bruno Kirby. Jack Palance was pretty old by then. He played a crazy, old cowboy named Curly who scares the heck out of everyone. That role brought him a little burst of fame, even though he was in his seventies by then. He did an Old Spice commercial where he mugged for the cameras and said, "Confidence is sexy . . . don't you think?" He looked crazy, but there was no questioning his confidence. His smile said it all. That was how it was with Rumsfeld, too. His whole worldview was summed up with that I'm-right-and-you're-not smile. He was splashed all over magazine covers. His briefings pulled in huge ratings. There were even reports of big increases in sales of the rimless glasses he wore. And I guess that for women closer to his age, that confidence-is-sexy thing held true, too.

"He's become such a pinup guy for older women that I've got a new nickname for him, Rumstud," President Bush told reporters in early 2002.

Maybe some of that went to his head. Maybe not. I think Donald Rumsfeld was very much being himself. It wasn't like he suddenly tried to come off as a tough guy. His persona is very much that of a military man—very hard-core and very abrupt. You don't have to watch your p's and q's. Donald Rumsfeld doesn't do that. He's a straight shooter. He tells you what's on his mind. That's admirable.

But I think Rumsfeld forgot something important after September 11. He forgot that anyone presenting himself as a national leader has to be able to come down to the common man's level. Confidence is good, but if you take it too far, if you become too full of yourself, you run the risk of losing touch. You have to be able to speak to the people. You have to treat congressmen and senators and even the media as equals. Watching Rumsfeld, sometimes it felt as if we were living in a dictatorship. He fell into an attitude of, "Don't question my authority. I'm tired of answering your stupid questions. I'm tired of your not getting what I am saying."

He should not have let his frustration get the better of him. He should have understood that he couldn't expect everyone to take him at his word on everything. He would never do that if he were in their shoes. He rubbed a lot of congressmen and senators the wrong way. He got so put out when people didn't immediately accept the urgency of what he was saying or when they asked him too many questions. But hold on, here. Congressmen and senators are elected to represent people, and that means asking important questions on their behalf. Donald Rumsfeld should have respected that more. He should have found the patience to answer more questions, and he should have remembered that even if they sounded to him like dumb questions, to a lot of people watching at home they might not have sounded dumb at all.

I'm not talking about the kind of thing we heard from the Susan Sarandons and Janeane Garofalos and Michael Moores of the world. Those were ridiculous, ludicrous questions they were raising in denouncing the war. They just wanted to raise trouble by bringing up a lot of nonsense. I'm not saying Rumsfeld should have had any patience with those people. Heck, no. But should he have shown a little more patience with elected officials just trying to do their jobs and represent their constituents? Absolutely. Rumsfeld needed to say, "Look, here what I know. Here's what you need to know. This is why it's urgent." He should have explained it to them in a way a child could understand.

He does not do that well. He does not come down to the common man's level very well.

Still, we have to think about what it was like to be Donald Rumsfeld during so crucial a stretch of U.S. history. He basically woke up every morning and heard the worst possible news he could hear about the dangers presenting themselves against our country. Every night before he went to bed, he would get updates that were even worse than what he had read that morning. It was a never-ending cycle. Rumsfeld was being fed a ton of top-secret information that even most senators and congressmen would not have known about. He had detailed, specific information about the terrorist threat that would have left just about any normal person with nightmares. It was that bad. He understood more about terrorism than the average layman could even conceive.

A lot of the negative feedback directed against Rumsfeld was just plain unfair when you consider that the man literally had to live in the mind-set of terrorists. He had to think like them. He had to be as crazy as them, to try to understand what they might cook up next. I don't think many Americans would be able to stay sane if they were asked to see and hear everything Donald Rumsfeld did about every last possible terrorist threat that our government has to guard against. He has gone through a massive education in the worst of human nature. He lives amid the ugly, the obscene, the unspeakable. People should cut him a little slack and keep in mind all the garbage he has had to study. Of course he's going to be a little short sometimes. Of course he's going to get agitated. That's only human nature. But sometimes he hurt himself.

If I could have sat down with Rumsfeld, I would have told him, "Look, you have to be a person, too, you can't just be a military leader. You have to give people a reason to want to understand what you're saying. You have to relate to them on a human level. You can't demand change without giving everyone a chance to understand the problem."

That sounds pretty basic. But Rumsfeld had the same problem again and again. He rubbed people the wrong way because he expected them to jump on the bandwagon on every last detail, even when they did not fully understand the urgency of the situation. You can't just yell at people to get them to accept what you're saying. You don't help them understand that way. That's like yelling at a kid and telling him he's stupid because he doesn't know that two plus two equals four. If he doesn't know, it's because he hasn't been taught math yet or not in a way he can understand.

Let's be blunt here. Part of the job is acting. Rumsfeld was used to the no-nonsense military style. He was used to everyone being on the same page. But in dealing with the press and senators and congressmen, sometimes it pays to go through the motions. You can listen to people, even if you don't agree with them and have no intention of changing your own thinking even a little bit. You can listen and say, "Okay, thanks," and even if it goes in one ear and out the other, so what? You're still going to gain some respect there, because you took the time to listen. Maybe you're thinking, This guy is talking a lot of crud here and I'm not going to listen to a word he says, but at least you're hearing him out. Sometimes acting cordial and polite makes a big difference.

That is something the Bush administration needs to reiterate about dealing with the press. Administration officials and their staff should be taught how to be more press savvy. They should be taught to be as patient as a mother is with a child. I understand it gets very frustrating when you are asked the same question fifty times and the audience still is not getting it. But maybe they're not getting it because you're not explaining it well enough. Maybe they're not getting it because you're being so impatient with them that they don't want to get it.

But you know what? As much as it would have helped the administration to treat the media and senators and congressmen with a little less disdain, I think Donald Rumsfeld himself had to be pretty much the way he was. Was it his job to make Americans happy? To feed them a rosy picture of the world that would make them feel better, even though it might not be accurate? Not for one second. His job has been to let the world know that he's not messing around. His job has been to let everyone know he's hell-bent on getting rid of terrorists and getting rid of dictators and getting rid of all the people who are in a position to harm our citizens or other people who can't protect themselves. That's what people need to understand.

It's a little crude, but Franklin Delano Roosevelt once described a Nicaraguan strongman by saying, "He may be an S.O.B., but he's *our* S.O.B." Sometimes you need a tough guy on your side who is unapologetic about being a tough guy. That's what I respect about Rumsfeld. He knows who he is. He's not out to win any popularity contests; he's not going to sugarcoat anything. He knows he has alienated a lot of people, and he knows there is no way to perform his mission without doing just that. He's not trying to position himself to run for president. He's doing what he has to do to perform a very tough job with distinction. He told himself, "This is what I'm good at, and this is what I'm going to do with my life. I'm not going to try to be a people pleaser. If some don't like me, tough luck."

I'm sure that Donald Rumsfeld will be remembered as a great military man who was a great leader in a time of need. He was the front man we needed. He defined our goals and our missions, and he scared the living heck out of terrorists around the world and out of any other people who don't like America. That was his job, not looking at opinion polls. His job was to keep us safe, and I think most people know he's done an amazing job of keeping this country safe. We may never known why he was sometimes so short, and so arrogant, because we will never know all the pressures he was under or all the doomsday intelligence briefings he had kicking around inside his head. But the bottom line is it didn't matter what we thought of Rumsfeld, it mattered what terrorists thought of Rumsfeld. I don't think a single terrorist out there ever had any doubt that Rumsfeld was going to do what he said he would do, and he was coming after them, not diplomatically but with bullets and bombs. Were terrorists scared of Rumsfeld? Yes! Did they respect him? Yes!

What mattered most was how Rumsfeld was seen in the rest of the world. I think the international community listened more closely to what he said than the national community did. People around the world knew that what he said was going to happen would happen. I liked that. He was extremely blunt, and when you're dealing with bad guys around the world, you need to be blunt. If some people saw that as arrogant, well, good. That is what we want. We want someone in that job who is always a little ticked off, someone who is a little cocky, someone who gets frustrated when other people dig in their heels and try to stop him. Would we rather have that or someone who is wishy-washy? Or someone who wants to get along with everybody? Or someone who wants to build a nice military résumé so he can use it to run for high office later?

Donald Rumsfeld never tried to be something he wasn't. He never tried to be a people pleaser or a poll watcher. He was never trying to impress people so they would want to push him to run for president. Rumsfeld loved his job. He loved keeping the country safe, and he was glad that he was the one entrusted with that huge responsibility rather than anyone else, because he was sure he could do a better job than anyone else. That's what separates a great leader from a mere politician. Even if you were put off by him, or disagreed with him, you could still see he was a great leader.

We needed someone hard-core to lead the fight against terrorism, and that's what we got in Rumsfeld. He should be remembered as a man who understood his job, and his mission, and did right by both. He did an amazing job of making others fear the consequences of their actions when it came to dealing with this country. That's what he was hired to do. And he did it. He wasn't hired to be a press secretary. He wasn't hired to be a comedian. He wasn't hired to make people smile and laugh. He was hired to keep this country safe. He was hired to be hard-nosed. And I don't think there's anyone out there, from terrorists to leftist movie stars, who could deny that Donald Rumsfeld was one heck of a hardnose.

CHAPTER 23

Dubya: My Kind of Redneck

When George Herbert Walker Bush tried to make himself out as a southerner, that was a stretch. He was a preppy, and he talked like one. He was an old-money blue blood born just outside of Boston. Can you get any less southern than that? Nope. I didn't buy it when the first President Bush tried to claim he was a southerner. But George W. Bush pulls it off. He walks the walk and more. I'd even have to say that he has a little redneck in him.

I mean that in a good way. It was pretty funny last fall when Howard Dean tried to suck up to southern men with all that talk about Confederate flags. To me, that was like Michael Dukakis strapping on that goofy-looking helmet and sitting in that tank. Politicians always look the most ridiculous when they are trying to be something they are not. Dukakis was a wimp's wimp. Here was a man who did not show the slightest trace of emotion when a journalist asked him how he would react if someone raped his wife. Dukakis didn't get mad at all. He was a brainy little wimp trying to act like a tough guy with that tank photo op, and it turned into a disaster for his campaign. Howard Dean is a northeast liberal all the way, a guy who ought to be sipping cappuccino in a Burlington café instead of trying to impress the good ole boys.

All Dean said was that he wanted "to be the candidate for guys with Confederate flags in their pickup trucks." What the heck is wrong with that? Shouldn't a man running for president want to be the candidate of *all* Americans? And shouldn't that include people in my part of the country, people from all walks of life? You bet. But once the liberals in the media grabbed onto that one, they were like a dog with a bone. There was no prying that one away from them. So Dean stepped up to the microphones looking as if he'd been crying all by himself in his room and said, "I deeply regret the pain that I may have caused."

No, what Dean deeply regretted was not having a clear sense of who he was as a candidate. He deeply regretted that he had not done a better job of faking some connection with southerners. The next thing you knew, he was telling us how bad the Confederate flag is. He was telling us how it's "a painful symbol and reminder of racial injustice and slavery." Well, of course it's all that. As if that's some kind of news flash. But it's much, much more than that. The real trouble starts when outsiders try to rip the Confederate flag loose from the context of life here in the South, just to score a few quick political points like Dukakis in that tank. As we like to say here in the South, that stuff don't fly.

George W. Bush doesn't have to fake anything to connect with those boys Howard Dean was trying to reach. I would say Bush is the ideal candidate for those boys. But you can find better symbols of that than the Confederate flag. Put it this way: Bush is the candidate for the guy who has a pickup truck and a gun in his gun rack and a tangle of fishing rods. A lot of people would call that a redneck. Is Bush a redneck? Not all the time. Can he be a redneck? Sure. He doesn't feel like he's above those situations, and that's why I think of him as a good ole boy. He doesn't feel like he's above a person. You can just tell a lot of these other candidates think they're above the average American.

You can take a southerner out of the South, but you can't take the South out of a real southerner. Sure, Bush was born in New Haven, Connecticut. Everyone knows that. And he went to prep school at Phillips Academy in Andover, Massachusetts, then went back to New Haven to study at Yale. And he later earned a business degree at Harvard. But at each stop along the way, he knew he was only doing his time among the Yankee elite, checking them out and learning their ways. He always saw himself as a southerner.

Growing up in the South is a big part of what makes Dubya truly southern. You have to live here when you're young. He was just a toddler when his dad loaded up the family Studebaker and drove off to West Texas to try to make it in the oil business. He spent his childhood in Midland, Texas, and went to Sam Houston Elementary School. He grew up around southerners, and that becomes a big part of your upbringing. You have the influence of the Bible Belt. You have the influence of church and the emphasis on family. But you also have the society as a whole that makes you southern. You kind of absorb the southern way of life.

"Midland was a small town, with small-town values," the president wrote in his book *A Charge to Keep*. "We learned to respect our elders, to do what they said, and to be good neighbors. We went to church. Families spent time together, outside, the grown-ups talking with neighbors while the kids played ball or with marbles and yo-yos. . . . No one locked their doors, because you could trust your friends and neighbors."

He said it was a happy childhood there in Midland, and it obviously stayed with him. Look at how much he loves Crawford, Texas. Who the heck has been to Crawford, Texas? Let's be honest. Who wants to retire there? But that's where George W. Bush is going to retire one day. He has taken a lot of criticism during his presidency for going back to Crawford so often and spending so much time there, but I'm all for it. He goes there to clear his mind and get back to his roots. You can never escape from the duties of the White House when you're president. That's just not a reality. The pressure follows you around wherever you are.

But spending time in Crawford seems to be good for him. That's where he feels he can be Dubya, instead of President Bush. He has a great time when he's down there. He feels comfortable with the people and the way of life. It's that mom-and-pop contentment and satisfaction people have with their own lives. They are not rich the way the way Bush family friends and neighbors are in Kennebunkport, Maine. They are rich because of their friendships, and their pride in their town, and their families.

I think that being southern is like a secret weapon for Bush. It's the key to his success. He connects with people because we southerners know how to do that. We're charming. We know when to crack a joke. We know when to back off a little, maybe, and give someone some room. You probably can't find two men who are more different than Bill Clinton and George W. Bush, but one thing they have in common is that they are both southern. They both have that southern folksiness. They know how to connect with real people. I don't think you are going to see many presidents elected from outside of the South. It's too big of an advantage in politics.

Do I think somebody like a Dick Cheney could become president? No, I don't. I don't think he connects with real people. George W. Bush has charisma, and he also has southern manners. He understands that you have to be a human being first and a president second. I think a lot of other people have missed that. They feel they have to act presidential all the time. They think they need to adopt a persona that makes them more like a leader. George W. Bush doesn't do that. He's proven he's a leader when we needed him to be, and we know he has leadership qualities. But there's a lot more to him than that. He can be a funny guy. He can be relaxed. He can be a human being before anything else. People criticized Bush for looking kind of scared and nervous when he gave that first press conference on September 11. Then later that day, back at the White House, he addressed the nation and looked presidential. But I think that made him real that we saw both sides of him that day.

Bush wears his emotions on his sleeve. He showed that with the war in Iraq and with September 11. And that is how most real people are, too. If you're frustrated, you tell people you're frustrated. You tell people you're upset. That is what a normal human being does. All these other candidates try to be so diplomatic and scripted, they don't ever seem human. If George W. Bush is ticked off, he usually lets you know it. Remember that time at a campaign event near Chicago during the 2000 campaign when Bush turned to Dick Cheney, thinking no microphones would catch what he was saying, and told him "There's Adam Clymer—major-league asshole—from the *New York Times*." That kicked up a big ruckus at the time; there was no question, it did not make Bush look very presidential. But that was human nature. Any one of us who found ourselves in his shoes would want to say something like that from time to time. Because Bush is southern, he can't help but be himself and be honest. It might hurt him in the short term, but over time, as the American people have gotten to know him, they see him as being a lot like they are.

Bush can connect with the guy who comes out to his ranch to fix his tractor on the farm, or the guy who works at the corner market, the same way he can connect with a Vicente Fox, the president of Mexico. Try to imagine someone like John Kerry striking up a conversation with the guy who works on John Deere tractors for a living. What a joke. That's something you can't fake. Bush can walk into any situation in any room and strike up a conversation. He understands the redneck point of view. He understands the farming type. He understands CEO types. He can communicate about people's concerns on a basic level, and that's something you either have or you don't have. No political handler can coach that. It's either there or it isn't.

Bush understands the importance of making a man feel like a man after he's done a hard job. That's kind of the mentality of George W. Bush.

He can find the enjoyment in pulling out a chain saw to cut down a tree himself even though he's president of the United States. Sure, he can afford to have a crew come in and cut down trees on his Crawford ranch and clear brush or whatever. But he's the kind of man who wants to do that himself. I'm sure his wife smiles and grins and kids him about it. That's what makes her love him. He's a real person. He's not the president all the time. He has to make tough decisions, but he can also go and chill out on the ranch. I think that's part of the southern mind-set. You don't always look at your time as how much it's worth.

That fits his love of sports, too. Bush was the boy playing football out in a field near his parents' house. He enjoys the outdoors and baseball. That was how he grew up. "I filled my days with baseball," he wrote in his book. "My first memories are of Midland, and when I think of growing up there, baseball comes to mind first. We were always organizing a game, in the schoolyard, or in the buffalo wallow behind my house on Sentinel Street. We played for hours, until our mothers would pull us away. I remember Mother yelling over the fence, insisting I had to come home for dinner, right now. Sometimes, on weekends, my dad would join us, impressing my friends by catching the ball behind his back."

Bush's father had been a good first baseman back at Yale, as most people know. His grandfather, Prescott Bush, batted cleanup for the Yale squad back in 1917. The family was always interested in sports. The Walker Cup golf tournament is named for his great-grandfather, George H. Walker, who was president of the U.S. Golf Association in 1920. Another great-grandfather, Samuel P. Bush, helped found the Ohio State University football team and served as a volunteer coach in 1892. Herbert Walker, an uncle, was one of the original owners of the New York Mets.

As a boy, George W. attended a Mets game with his uncle, and a love of baseball has been a lifelong theme. He and his boyhood friends would play all the time. I think Bush really came into his own when he became part owner of the Texas Rangers; he would sit right behind home plate, signing George W. Bush baseball cards and handing them to anyone who asked. Bush didn't have much luck back at Yale, and he only played a little on the freshman team, but, in Texas, the players liked him. They accepted him as almost one of their own.

That might be a good way to think of Bush, as a Texas ballplayer. He became friends with Nolan Ryan, the great pitcher, when he was with the Rangers, and Ryan inspired so many other great ballplayers. So many of these big, strapping, hard-throwing pitchers have come out of Texas, it's easy to lose count. Nolan and Roger Clemens and Kerry Wood and now Josh Beckett, who came out of nowhere to pitch the Florida Marlins to a World Series championship. Pitchers in the Ryan tradition are known for their good fastballs, their fearlessness on the mound, and their willingness to throw a ball high and tight to intimidate a batter. That to me sounds a lot like George W. Bush.

Another mark of a true southern man is having respect for God and respect for women. You can tell how much respect George W. Bush has for his daughters, wife, and mother. Just look at the way he treats Condoleezza Rice. The National Organization for Women and all those nuts out there in the women's movement stereotyped the South as a place where men want to put women in their place, making babies and cooking the food on top of giving up a career. That is not what the South is about. Southerners aren't against women having a career. We've gotten a bad rap. Look, I'm all for women having a career. Southerners, in general, are for women having careers. We also understand that there's nothing wrong with choosing to stay home and raise kids, because that's one of the most important jobs anyone can have.

Southern people as a whole emphasize family. But that doesn't mean women are supposed to be mothers only. The South has come a long way. Women can be independent and have their own careers. But we are a lot more family-oriented than northerners are. If you're southern, and you know who all your cousins and aunts and uncles and grandparents are, you hang out with them. If people want to joke about that, and say the state motto in Arkansas should be "Eight million people with eight last names," they don't know the South.

The South is a mind-set. We're much more friendly, much more happy, and much more content with our way of life than a lot of people in the North. We're brought up to have manners. You open the door for a lady. You scoot out a chair for a lady. You don't back talk your mother. If you ever back talk your mother, you're going to get "talked to" by your father. Southerners are brought up with a mind-set to respect others and to be friendly and kind. If I'm in a line at the grocery store and somebody is behind me, I'm not going to pick up a magazine and alienate myself. I'm going to talk to the person and ask how he's doing.

That just feels natural to us in the South, and what's wrong with that? I mean, when was the last time you heard of someone being shot for opening the door? Or someone being stabbed because they said "Good day" or "How's your day been?" Being kind is part of the southern upbringing. I would much rather be that way than be in New York and, after a day, become so numb that when I bump into someone I wouldn't even say "Excuse me" or "Sorry." That's how it is in the North. It's such a fast-paced life, and you're the only person who matters.

I was brought up as a southern gentleman. And being a southern gentleman is based around God and the Bible and respecting women. I think that's why you see so many southern gentlemen who have come to greatness because they respect women. They're nice to women. They open doors for them. They want to do things for women and not because they think they're above them. That's how they have been brought up by their mothers and their grandmothers and their dads. A southerner is comfortable with faith. He's not afraid to claim religion as part of his platform. And that is another reason why George W. Bush has been able to connect so well with people. They trust him when he talks about his faith. They know he grew up in the South, where religion is a strong influence.

I hope we never lose the southern mind-set. I hope it spreads all over the country. Lord knows some places up north need it. My dad was born in North Dakota, and you don't get much more northern than that. I love the North. But I truly never want to leave my southern heritage. I am sick and tired of all the stereotypes of southern people as a bunch of hillbillies. No, we don't use shotguns to go and kill our food. Yes, we do have fast-food places, and we even have nice restaurants. We actually have shoes. We are not a bunch of inbreeds. We don't live in trailers. Northerners have the mentality that the South is like the butt hole of America, and it's not.

I'm proud to be southern. We had a bad rap in the South for being bigots or racists. But that's gone. That was the Old South. Now the southern mind-set revolves around being polite and courteous, and that's what makes the South great. It's not the history of slavery, not the history of plantations, and not the history of tobacco farming or cotton picking or whatever stereotype you want to throw out there. That's not what the South is anymore. For people who criticize the South, I say, "Come down and see us, and then see how much you criticize us."

CHAPTER 24

Where Is America Going?

ike a lot of you out there, I am worried about where this country is headed. We are moving into a period in American history that many good people everywhere will agree is just disgusting. Soon enough gay marriage will be a reality. Soon enough Janet Jackson flashing us at the Super Bowl will be the least of our worries on TV. Why is all this happening? How has the country changed so much for the worse in the last few years? The answer is simple. Conservatives have stopped fighting for what they believe in.

We can't let this trend continue. It's time for us to band together and stop worrying about just ourselves. We have to start worrying about the future of this country. Every American believes in something, right? Well, the time has come to get out there and fight for what you believe in. Speaking personally, my goal for the future is to make a difference with the things I believe in. I can't do that alone, though. You can't do it alone, either. But together, we can make a difference. We need to get back in the game, instead of just warming the bench.

Most of us work at least three months out of the year just to pay our taxes. Then on top of that we pay sales taxes almost every day. But how many of us take the time to vote, let alone pay attention to what's going on in this country? Not nearly enough, and we all know it. That is how passive we are as a nation. We give more money to the government than to any other organization and we don't even care what they do with it? I care and you should, too.

We are scared of all the powerful people in Washington, but why? We are the ones who vote all these stupid congressmen and senators into office. So without us they don't have a job! It's that simple. They work for us. Their job is to represent you and me and your neighbor Bill and your cousin Evelyn and everyone else, too. Now ask yourself this question: When was the last time you wrote a letter to a member of Congress, or picked up the phone and called, or even just sent an e-mail? I bet most of you cannot remember the last time you did that. See what I am saying here? It's our fault this country has gone off the moral road. We are the drivers, and it looks to me as if we have fallen asleep at the wheel. Elected officials are smart. They know we are scared of them and intimidated by them. They know we don't get involved because we are too preoccupied with our personal lives to worry about them. This is why we are lost as a nation.

We have to remind ourselves that taking an active interest in our country and where it's going is a basic foundation of life, just as basic and essential as committing ourselves to church and family. The three should go together. Can we please put politics back into religion? Why is it that churches around America no longer talk about world issues from the pulpit? If I had a dollar for every time I heard a pastor say, "Don't mix politics and the Bible," I would be rich. We all need to have a moral compass. I get mine from my faith, and I think that goes for a lot of you out there, too. So why on earth would we want our religious leaders to put their heads in the sand and pretend the whole dirty world of politics doesn't exist or is somehow beyond them? I guess it's because there is a fear that someone in the audience might be offended if the pastor says something political.

The truth always makes someone angry. But if you are offended, more than likely you have a malfunction in your moral compass. There is nothing wrong with offending some people now and then. That's good. It helps keep them awake. If the pastor wants to use his time on Sunday to talk about the war in Iraq, or the demise of corporate America, then he should absolutely do that. We are so scared of offending people that we have just walked away from serious conversations about the issues of the day. Well, we need to start talking about those issues, and we had better hurry, too. If we don't, we just might open our eyes one day and find that we no longer recognize this great country.

I hope I haven't scared you. There is room for hope. There is always room for hope. But only if we all wake up and get more involved. It doesn't have to be difficult. Heck, you can even make it fun, my friends. Do yourselves a favor and pull out a pen or a pencil right now and write down just two things you want to see changed in this country. Did you do that yet? Good, now spend a few minutes thinking about what you can do to make some kind of difference on the two things you've written down. Start by making a little noise. Call the people who are supposed to represent you in government. Make sure they know just how you feel about the issues, and remind them that there are many people who share your convictions. You might even find the experience rewarding. Don't just read this book and say, "Hey, that was fun, I'm going to have to listen to this Ben Ferguson on the radio or catch him on TV." No, read this book, and if it stirs you up, if it makes you angry or passionate, then do something with that anger and passion.

The bottom line is if we don't get the ball rolling right away for this generation, there might not be a ball left to roll for the next one. It scares me to think about what this country must look like from the outside. But you and I both know how great it really is and how much better it can become. I hope this book sends a clear message to the Republican Party that they need to start listening and engage the average American and especially the younger generation. I don't like the way the Republicans treat the average conservative, but that does not mean I don't agree with their beliefs. It's time for the Republicans to open their eyes and let a new generation in on the future of the party. If they don't, then before you know it, most of America will find another party that will listen to them. That's what scares me more than anything.

I hope this book has inspired you. I hope it has made you angry in a good way. I hope it makes you want to get more involved. But even more than that I hope it has helped you find your moral compass. We all know how important it is to believe in something. Let's face it: If you don't, then you are liable to fall for anything. If each of us can look inward and decide what really makes us tick, that will put us on a path to a successful life. That sounds simple, but most people I see in politics have lost their moral compass. That's why you see them vote with the special interests and corporate America. That's why they sell out to anyone and everyone. We need to stop that, and it's up to my generation. But we need you—the older generation—to step up to the plate and lead by example. We need you to set an example about the importance of knowing who you are and what you stand for and what your most deeply held beliefs are. That has to happen, because without a moral compass we will one day be referred to as a country of people that used to be great. Call me selfish, but I want this country to be the greatest forever.